By the Author

When Towns Had Walls: Life in a Medieval English
Town

Home Sweet Home in the Nineteenth Century

Warriors' Weapons

When Towns Had Walls

WHEN TOWNS

Walter Buehr

HAD WALLS

Life in a
Medieval English Town

THOMAS Y. CROWELL COMPANY
NEW YORK   *Established 1834*

Editorial Consultant: Text, Jane Jordan Browne

Manufactured in the United States of America

L.C. Card 76-106585

ISBN 0-690-88179-7

1 2 3 4 5 6 7 8 9 10

Contents

When Towns Had Walls

Introduction

How do we know about the life and times of men and women who lived almost six hundred years ago? For one thing people have always written about what was happening around them, either in an official capacity or quite unofficially, and what they have written tells us what they thought and how they lived.

The last decades of the fourteenth century and the first of the fifteenth, the period covered in this book, were rich in imaginative literature. It is the historian's good fortune that the two greatest English poems of the age were magnificent social documents as well. Geoffrey Chaucer's *The Canterbury Tales* has been equally praised as a literary masterpiece and as a brilliant re-creation of fourteenth-century English society. The Canterbury Pilgrims (there are twenty-nine in all, from knight to plowman) represent an England of castle, field, and town. Their be-

1

havior and the stories they tell are even more revealing than Chaucer's minutely detailed description of their appearance. What better picture could we want of a merchant than the one Chaucer gives us? In the Prologue we first meet this canny townsman with his French beaver hat and daintily buckled boots, "so expert at currency exchange none knew he was in debt." Later "The Merchant's Tale," a wry condemnation of matrimony, gives point to his anguished complaints of marriage to a shrew.

The other remarkable poem of this general period is the vigorous satire *The Vision of William Concerning Piers the Plowman*. Credited to Will Langland, a cleric with a strong moral bent and a biting tongue, this poem is the best word-picture extant of the lives of peasants and poor townsmen. The works of such minor moral poets as John Gower and John Lydgate reinforce the scene, particularly of corruption in government and Church.

Popular literature reflects contemporary beliefs, tastes, and manners. The French romances and the English poems *Sir Gawain and the Green Knight* and the *Alliterative Morte d'Arthur* are galloping good stories that also define a code of behavior in the castle and on the battlefield. The homely and realistic *fabliaux* and fables (stories of beasts with human attributes) are mirrors of the temperament,

2

domestic mores, virtues, and goals of the rising merchant class.

In English professional literature two works stand out: John of Arderne's *Fistula in Ano* discusses the practice and conduct of a medieval physician; Henry de Bracton's thirteenth-century textbook of English common law is a milestone in the history of jurisprudence.

Fourteenth- and fifteenth-century literature abounds in less studious manuals of instruction. "Books of Nurture" like *The Babees Book* and *The Book of the Knight of La Tour-Landry* outline model conduct for young squires or daughters of noble households—advice much in demand by rich townsmen who aped their social betters. Another book of counsel—written in 1394 by a bourgeois known as The Goodman of Paris, to instruct his young wife on how to conduct herself and her household—is a wealth of moral advice, and of practical hints on gardening, cooking, serving, hiring servants, making a husband happy, and keeping insects at bay. Cookbooks like *The Forme of Cury* (cooking) inform us what the medieval man thought was tasty and what food was available for him to taste. The collections of domestic letters that have come down to us reveal the heart of family life, from money crises to marriage plans.

Official literature of this period is generally of two kinds: formal works, such as historical chronicles and encyclopedias, and royal, ecclesiastical, and municipal records. The first great chroniclers were members of the clergy, and in England Thomas Walsingham of St. Albans, a Benedictine abbey, continued this tradition from the end of the reign of Edward III into the fifteenth century. John of Trevisa translated the Benedictine Ranulf Higden's *Polychronicon* as well as the chatty thirteenth-century encyclopedia *On the Properties of Things,* compiled by Bartholomew Anglicus, a Franciscan. Secular history came into its own with the Crusades, especially with Jean Froissart, a French chronicler at the court of Queen Philippa. In his famous pages, which cover the years from 1326 to 1400, the pageantry of court life and brilliant military victories spring to life. Layamon's *Brut* (1205), a homelier chronicle of English history, was picked up in the fourteenth century and continued by another native historian. These formal histories portrayed the national and international scene; for life that was unique to the town, we must consult official records.

Every town had its Red Book or Black Book or White Book, in which were listed all the customs and privileges of the town in the form of statutes, writs, and charters. The town's Day Books or Letter-Books recorded matters of interest to the municipality. There were also the proceedings of Parliament and other royal law courts and agencies throughout the realm, the guild ordinances of the town, as well as individual bookkeeping accounts, wills, testaments, and reports of taxations on personal property.

We learn lively history from these dry-as-dust documents. The Red Books and Black Books and White Books tell us how and why the town grew; the Day Books, its perennial problems, such as the threat of fire and poor sanitation. Law-court proceedings and guild ordinances offer insights into the administration of law and justice, and the workings of a supervised economy. Merchants' account books record such ordinary business as the price a burgher paid a carpenter to build his house and the specifics for its construction. Wills inventory houses room by room, and tax records list every item of a householder's property down to the wool on his wife's distaff.

This period can be reconstructed from more than words, for much visual evidence remains. Illuminations painstakingly brushed by monks in scriptoriums to adorn Bibles and prayer books portray a rich medieval scene. The magnificent *Luttrell Psalter* shows the plowman in his fields, the noble at table, and the traveling tinker with his pack of wares.

5

Tapestries and stained-glass windows, intricately carved choir stalls or church statuary, although religious in subject matter, reflect their own times in every other detail. Tomb effigies costume those they honor in death as they were in life.

Archaeology has unearthed tangible relics of the past. A cache of fourteenth-century clothes discovered in Iceland revealed how garments were cut and sewn together. The less perishable objects of daily life, like brass and silver utensils, furniture, and armor, were handed down from generation to generation. Some old towns live still, though they remain in a state of greater preservation on the Continent than they do in England, and archaeologists have literally peeled back the centuries in domestic dwellings in Pembridge in Haverfordshire to find them as they were in the fourteenth century.

Using all these sources we have been able to reconstruct individual, family, house, shop, and town. The social historian need not be overly narrow; when applicable to the period described, we have borrowed the meticulous observations of Alexander of Neckham, a twelfth-century wandering cleric, and the graphic descriptions of his contemporary, Theophilus, a Benedictine artist-monk who practiced various arts and sciences. Similarly, we have copied sketches drawn in the sixteenth century, when they show craftsmen at work much as they were 150 years earlier.

Since the historian of the medieval period does not have a complete picture, he must choose the particular incident and call it typical. This is what we have done. To describe life in a medieval walled town in the later Middle Ages, we have created one. The town is Norcaster, a prosperous self-governing community in the county of Norfolk, a part of England once called East Anglia. Although there is no Norcaster on any map of England old or new, town and townsfolk are real inasmuch as their story has been drawn from the records of other towns and other people that did exist.

The years 1377 to 1422 were distressing years for England. Richard II, who reigned from 1377 to 1399, proved capricious as well as extravagant. The Wars with France, begun in 1337, stretched past the mid-fifteenth century. Despite several glorious military victories, the Wars gained no territory for England except Calais, and brought violence in the train of financial hardship. A bankrupt government had to rely on military retainers, and by enriching the fighting nobility, temporarily set their power above the crown's. During the long truces that characterized the Wars, armed and idle bands of men terrorized the populace and turned justice to their own advantage.

The Church suffered from corruption and discord within, and from heresy without. The papal schism of 1378 produced rival popes in Avignon and Rome, and it was not until 1417 that a single acceptable pope, Martin V, was elected to rule a unified Church. John Wycliffe and his followers, the Lollards, disgusted by the abuses of a too-worldly clergy, led a movement that rocked the foundation of Catholic orthodoxy. The Black Death, plagues from Asia, which first hit England in 1438–39, broke out five times again in the course of the century, devastating the population and bringing in their wake economic and social upheaval.

But from chaos and disaster new life emerged. The Wars with France and the papal scandal encouraged a spirit of nationalism in England, which helped dissolve local loyalties. An aggressive royal government was able to limit the authority of feudal barons and bishops, while it encouraged the growth and representative strength of a middle class grown prosperous on sheep farming and trade in wool and cloth. As the feudal world lay dying, a modern urban society was born. The towns brought wealth and civilization to the kingdom, as town life brought wisdom and self-reliance to its citizens. Let us see how one town grew and how its citizens flourished with it, in knowledge and love of liberty and a sense of national destiny.

In 1377, the first year of Richard II's reign, Norcaster was a rightly famous borough. The liberties it afforded and the prosperous trade it encouraged had made it the tenth largest town in England. Within and without, its walls, cottages, and lanes teemed with lusty, brave, and brawling folk who loved good food and drink, often better than they loved God, and feared the loss of freedom perhaps more than they dreaded the Devil's wiles.

FIELD SCENE

Norcaster

1

As the eastern sky grew pink on a summer day in the late Middle Ages, a stern silhouette of towers and crenellated battlements emerged from the morning mists. For some travelers that day it was their first view of the walled town of Norcaster that for over 1,200 years had lain beside the banks of a small river in northeastern England.

As the sun rose higher, even those several leagues away could hear trumpets sound shrilly from the towers alongside the four main gates. Those eager marketfolk already at the gates listened to the sergeants-at-arms pushing open the creaking timber doors to let them pass inside.

From within the walls, dogs barked, roosters crowed, and pigs squealed as they were driven from their pens. Shutters banged open and children clattered down stone steps to let down their water buckets into the town's wells. Smoke from newly stirred fires rose from chimneys and roof lanterns while housewives berated lazy apprentices for lying

11

abed. Norcaster had awakened to a new day.

The busiest approach to the town was by the London road. The traveler passed furrowed fields full of peasants in flat-brimmed hats tilling the dark earth, their woolen smocks hitched up, showing their cloth stockings. From time immemorial the fields had been divided into narrow furlong strips, and still at the end of the fourteenth century the farmer, with help from his sons, turned shallow furrows into ridges, marking his own acres with an oxen-drawn plow. Behind him his wife scattered seed from a bag slung over her shoulder, measuring the grain with her hand and regulating her cast with the rhythm of footfalls. In the thirteenth century enough arable land had been claimed from the waste to adopt a three-field system of planting. Two fields provided a winter crop of rye and wheat, and spring crops of beans, barley, or oats, while animals were turned out to graze on harvest stubble and to fertilize the third field, which lay fallow. The fields were rotated one by one to increase their productivity. Meadowlands supplied pastures for cattle and sheep, while one outfield was always planted with teasels, the fuller's thistle, so necessary to the clothworkers' craft.

Arable land existed all around the circuit of the wall, but to the northeast, past the banks of the river Bure, in sharp contrast to the orderly fields lay the

12

marshlands, a swampy mass of reeds, dotted with bright lavender and yellow marsh flowers and nests of cranes, bitterns, and ducks. But this fen was also fruitful, for border acres could be drained and farmed, and the rest provided rushes for the floors of houses and wild fowl for the table. It even provided amusement, for when the marsh ponds froze, town boys skimmed on horsebone skates fastened securely to their boots and challenged each other with wooden staffs.

East of the town lay the woods, reached by means of paths. It, too, had grown smaller year by year as timber was cut and the waste claimed for pasturage. Here, still within reach of the townsmen, were badgers, rabbits, foxes, martins, and polecats. In the forest depths roamed wild boar and deer, reserved for the pleasure of the king and nobles.

The Bure was the same river that flowed into the sea at Yarmouth, once the great fishing port of East Anglia. Waterways were the chief means of transport in medieval times. Norcaster's common barge, poled or dragged by donkey teams along the riverbanks, exported the work of the town's craftsmen, often returning with a cargo of salted herring from Yarmouth; ships of the Merchant Adventurers brought goods from farther afield. Between the great stone bridge spanning the Bure and a smaller one of timber at the east end of the ramparts, wharves and warehouses were strung along the muddy banks. These were used for unloading and storing large shipments of grain, flax, salt, and wool. Clusters of dories were usually moored alongside the docks and river stairs that gave access to the town.

The river current ran fast enough to turn the wheels of four water mills within the town's boundaries. One was constructed on a floating hull fastened to a bridge arch. Travelers entering the town by Bridgegate would have seen the miller

NETTING RIVER FISH

standing atop a platform to pour grain down over the millstones, which ground away as the mill wheels churned. When a boat came, the platform was lifted to let it pass.

Fish traps and enclosures built in several places along the riverside also inhibited the freedom of the waterway. Carp, eel, and tench thrived despite the pollution. Though the council imposed a stiff fine of ten shillings for throwing refuse in the Bure, the tanners and the butchers continued to be offenders, and no one thought of removing the public latrines at the river gates. Despite these impediments, traffic was fairly heavy on the Bure, for it joined the Great Ouse at Lynn, and the Ouse, from its source deep in Oxfordshire, wandered through the East Midlands. Tolls of passage were a good source of revenue for the town. Early in the thirteenth century the lord of the neighboring manor stopped passage on the Bure and collected tolls for himself; but the borough appealed to the crown, and its ancient rights were upheld.

Through the centuries, as the acreage within the walls became more and more crowded, the boundaries of Norcaster expanded to include land and important buildings. The land of several neighboring manors was mixed with the borough's. The pastures that the borough originally shared with bishops and

15

barons slowly passed into the hands of the powerful town corporation. The lords did not press their claims, and Norcaster gained more than five hundred acres in this way. Various orders of monks were also attracted to the town. The priory of the Austin Canons, called the Holy Trinity, well established by the end of the twelfth century, stood like a cathedral amid the cottages. The friars' relations with council and commons had always been good, unlike those between other monasteries and towns. These monks differed from those of more secluded orders. They did parish work and were blessed for their gentle ministrations to the old and infirm. In their hospital a hundred sick could be cared for at one time, though several were bundled in one bed. In 1349 they had ceded some of their land for a public burying ground. More than a third of the town had perished in the first strike of the Plague, and there had been no place for them in consecrated ground.

The Franciscans, too, had a substantial convent and church to the south outside the walls. No one could remember when the followers of St. Francis of Assisi had come to Norcaster, but shortly after 1224 a worthy noble had given them an acre in the poorest part of town. The friars did not complain, for their creed was to own no property, and they

16

lived humbly from day to day on the charity of the town. The Grayfriars, as they were called, had come into the world to save souls, and the religious revival they sparked won the hearts of the people who hated the clerical abuses they saw around them. The Franciscans' humility laid bare the selfish concerns of wealthy clergy and the oppression of the ecclesiastical courts.

The Grayfriars' popularity, however, proved their downfall. Soon they preempted the financial support of the parish priests, and merchants and nobles began to vie for the prayers of the holy men. Then a papal bull was issued allowing them to "possess" as long as they did not consider themselves to "own." As the Franciscans became rich, they left Christ for the convent. Their new "possessions" cost money to keep up, and they had to resort to sending out limiters or professional beggars to dredge contributions from each ward of the town. Their sisters in Christ, the cloistered Poor Clares, retained their innocence. From a convent not far from the Grayfriars' church, they worked a market garden and a dairy and kept bees.

Not all of the large buildings outside the town were religious. For the convenience of travelers who wanted to avoid the gate tolls, several inns had been built outside the city gates. The most famous of these was St. Botolph's, named for a sixth-century patron saint of wayfarers. Like others inns, St. Botolph's consisted of a courtyard bounded by galleries into which a number of rooms opened. Guests slept on beds stacked one above another like ships' bunks.

It may seem amazing that such important business was going on outside the walls, but the fact is that English towns had less need for protection than Continental ones, and in truth the boundaries of the borough had never been defined by the ramparts. The Saxons abhorred the Roman-built walls as graves of freedom, and they raised timber houses in the open fields. Despite constant wars, first with the Danes, later with the French and Scots, and perennial raids by neighboring barons, suburbs sprang up and endured. Once a year, on the vigil of the Ascension, the freemen walked the bounds of the township, belaboring each other with sticks. Afterward they gathered in the marketplace to hear the town clerk recount the ordinances and liberties of the borough. The "beating of the bounds" served to remind them of their hard-won liberties.

For many, the protective walls of Norcaster were the symbol of the town, because they distinguished between those who had market privileges and those who did not. Little remained of the age-old masonry;

18

DEFENDING THE TOWN

only the flat Roman bricks around the thick base bore witness to the first conquerors of Britain. Time and again the walls had crumbled and been rebuilt. The Viking raids in the ninth century had won East Anglia to the Danelaw, and succeeding centuries saw constant struggles for supremacy between the kings of Wessex and the Danes. After the Conquest, the Norman barons refortified the ramparts, and the scare of the French Wars prompted Edward III to have them repaired again. At the end of the fourteenth century the walls rose about twenty feet, with a circumference of a little more than a mile and three quarters. As in most military defenses of this period the parapets were surmounted by crenellations and strengthened at intervals with semicircular bastions, the largest of which guarded the four main gates.

Besides Broadgate at the London road, Bridgegate, and Aldgate to the east, there was the western St. Botolph's Gate. The Roman name is lost, and the Anglo-Saxons called it Heafod or Head Gate, but for as long as the town could remember, it had been St. Botolph's. The same name was given to the inn and the chapel by the hermitage and to the holy well on the western road. Both Broadgate and Bridgegate had central arches eleven feet wide, and two smaller lateral arches. Within the bastions that projected over the walls were the guard rooms. There were still other gates: Fieldgate and Rivergate, Friarsgate and Fordgate, whose names tell us where they led. These were smaller, postern gates, and though some were equipped with towers, they were neither the principal entrances nor defenses of the town.

The ramparts of Norcaster must have been an imposing sight to any would-be attackers—a stern bulwark of buff-colored limestone, fortified by towers, rising higher where the ground sloped upward and further protected by a deep ditch or moat on all sides but the north, where the river ran. The ditch was fed by streams from the fields and had to be continually cleared of debris in order to serve its defensive purpose. To aid in defense, the top of the wall was pierced with loopholes, and a wooden railed gallery two feet wide circled inside the ramparts. Here, in time of battle, bowmen stood ready to loose their arrows or gunners to fire their hand-cannon. The early hand-firearms, which were short-barreled matchlocks fitted at the end of a pole, had a terrific recoil, but the rail kept the town guard from falling backward. Sometimes the loopholes held iron balls with a hole in the center large enough to let pass an arrow from a longbow. After the townsman fired, he would turn the ball to one side to protect himself from being shot by the enemy.

The barbicans or towers that protected the vulnerable gates were built very tall and fitted with a double drawbridge and iron gratings called portcullises, which could be hauled up vertical stone grooves by a system of pulleys. These towers were the mainstay of the town's outer defenses. Their semicircular shape and open-topped fighting platforms allowed the garrison to fight from several directions, shooting sideways through slits in the masonry. Through openings in the floor they could pour fire, boiling liquids, and stones on invaders.

Enemies, however, had a number of devious ways to attack such a well-defended town. Sappers addressed themselves to the walls, undermining them or using battering rams to make them crumble. Engines of war made of springs, weights, and rope, such as mangonels, arbalests, or catapults, like massive crossbows, could hurl stones, dead horses, or fireballs over the ramparts. A moat filled with grain or logs made a bridge out of an impassable ditch. If the enemy couldn't get under or through, he tried to climb over. With ladders men could scale walls, while wall-high wooden siege-towers on wheels were moved up under a smoke screen. But a really well-fortified town like Norcaster would have had to be starved into surrender through a long siege.

Of course the town was always on watch against

A TOWNSMAN SHOOTS THROUGH
A PROTECTED LOOPHOLE.

aggressors. Repairing the walls, clearing the ditch, and patrolling the parapet were major responsibilities of the burgesses. The freemen of the guilds took turns keeping watch and ward over the town day and night. A salaried sergeant-at-arms occupied the chambers in each of the four main towers. According to the Assize of Arms first established in 1181, every townsman provided his own arms according to his station in life. Twice a year a nationwide call to muster determined who was liable for military service. Wars were continuous in Scotland, France, and Wales, and most kings had to contend with rebellious barons. In 1385, when Edward III had called every able-bodied man in the kingdom to fight the French, the poor went forth with cudgel and pike in their gambesons or heavily padded leather jackets. Others took crossbow or longbow, and the rich were armored in hauberk, basinet, and gauntlets and carried sword and buckler. The basinet was a helmet, and gauntlets, metal gloves. The hauberk was body armor, which earlier had been made of metal mesh and lined with felted animal fur. By the 1400's plate armor was replacing chain metal, especially on arms and legs.

Attacks were infrequent during the years 1377 to 1422. Most of those who approached the town were not enemies but came on a welcome mission, to bring

goods to barter in the marketplace. From a distance
they could see the town rise above the ramparts.
Spires and towers of churches and the gabled roofs
of thatch and tile made a jagged line against the
sky. Here and there poked a few conical roofs of the
eleventh century, a reminder of the Norman trading
colony that had flourished here. Above all reared the
massive head of the Norman keep or castle, which existed before Henry I came to the English throne.
Looking down from the wall on 119 acres of buildings, gardens, and waste places, one could see that
the streets were more orderly than in other medieval
towns. The Romans had laid out the town like a
parallelogram, with two main streets crossing each
other in the center of town. They led from the four
great gates and marked the town into wards. The
position of the gates had not changed in twelve and
a half centuries, so the basic Roman plan remained
intact, even though Norcaster had its share of dark
and tortuous lanes. The general prospect of the town,
at least from atop the ramparts, was pleasing. The
Norman keep dominated the scene, but there were
more than thirty churches, many of them imposing
edifices, and a splendid guildhall. One colorful house
and garden after another straggled from wall to wall.
The vivid yellow, blue, and red decorations of these
two- and three-story houses showed bright against

their dark oak frames folded in with whitewashed plaster.

The Norman keep, like all fortresses of that period, had been built for military purposes. Situated midtown on the edge of a hill and enclosed by an earthwork surmounted by a timber palisade, the keep itself was a rough rectangle. Its walls were solid masonry up to the ceiling of the first story, built from stone filched from the Roman walls. In the fourteenth century it was used as a prison where felons were kept until tried, and also as a storehouse for ammunition—saltpeter, pellet powder, and cannon balls.

The reason for the great number of churches in the town was that Norcaster was not the see of a bishop, and that the two powerful religious centers, the abbey of the Austin Canons and the convent of the Franciscans, had not been established until rather late. Before the Conquest there were only eight parish churches, but the Normans added more than a dozen to these. Some churches remained little more than chapels, but others were added to or rebuilt until they took the usual form of a Christian cross, with a long central aisle or nave, intercepted by lateral arms. These Norman churches were sturdy and dignified, supported by massive pillars within and buttressed without, their square Romanesque towers rising above the transept, which crossed the nave.

The three most important churches in Norcaster were Holy Rood, Holy Trinity, and the Church of St. George. St. George was the oldest, most restored, and largest church within the walls. When rebuilt after the Great Fire, as Norcastrians called the conflagration of 1359, it could accommodate one quarter of the population. The reconstruction lasted from 1362 to 1417, prosperous years for the town and glorious years for architecture. At St. George rose again from its Norman base, it soared in Gothic splendor. Medieval builders rarely copied older styles; they designed in the fashion of the time. Even the two new towers flanking the west end differed in style; the southern was in decorated Gothic surmounted by a spire, the northern, the last to be completed, was Perpendicular. All forms of Gothic, early or late, aimed at loftiness and lightness. The architectural features of St. George made it seem to float upward—from the multi-shafted piers of Purbeck marble to the high, pointed nave arches, and upward still to the arch-framed windows in the clerestory and the intricate ribbed vaulting of the ceiling.

We see only the shells of medieval churches today, so it is hard to imagine what they looked like in the fourteenth century. The larger churches and cathedrals were divided into western and eastern parts—the nave, and the chancel, which included the choir, sanctuary, and apse. The nave belonged to the people; the rest was the domain of the clergy, kept from layfolk's view by a rood screen, an openwork partition spanning the nave at the entrance to the chancel. Though layfolk never saw the main altar, they had their own, situated between two doors of the rood screen, with a crucifix suspended above.

In the choir west of the rood screen rose still another structure called a pulpitum, whose stairs the priest mounted to recite the epistle and gospel at Mass. The altar and communion table stood in the sanctuary, and here, too, relics were kept. The clergy of St. George zealously guarded its holy treasures— portions of the stone tablets on which God wrote the law for Moses with his finger, and hairs of St. Thomas of Canterbury enclosed in a little ivory box with a knob of copper.

In St. George an apse with fan vaulting extended behind the glittering main altar. This was a semicircular projection built to answer the need for extra altars and chapels. It was the fashion in the fourteenth century for fraternities of craftsmen called guilds to pay for priests to say prayers in a private chapel, and to donate gold and silver vessels and brocaded vestments for his use. This was known as endowing a chantry.

The interior of St. George's was glorified by artists who praised their creator in their work. The walls, ceilings, screens, statues, and choir stalls were skillfully carved or painted and gilded in bright colors. Aisles gleamed with brass effigies of the rich merchants of Norcaster, while light from stained-glass windows of the clerestory and the great circular east window bathed the stone walls in soft hues.

The guildhall, newly enlarged in the last decade of the fourteenth century by the Corpus Christi Guild, bordered the town square. The upper story, where the town council met, was supported on arches, which opened onto the marketplace, a scene of constant hustle and bustle.

From the beginning the marketplace was the heart of the town, where the four main streets converged in an open space as large as a city block. This square was used for many purposes. In earlier days the townsfolk assembled here to attend the hundred court, and here the women still gathered to draw water from the conduit, or "standard," which carried it fresh from streams outside the walls. On feast days the folk crowded around the cockfighting pit and every day indulged in the grimmer amusement of taunting the culprits fastened in the stocks or pillory, common medieval engines of punishment.

But always, and especially, the marketplace was

29

just that, a place to buy and sell. The first market in Norcaster had been held in the lower story of a porch built onto St. George. Later a market cross was set up in the midst of the square, a cross-shaped stone edifice raised on a flight of stone stairs and topped by a lead-covered, pointed roof supported by timber posts to protect the market folk from inclement weather. The town's weights and measures were kept here in plain view. Later, when the guildhall was erected, a great beam, or weighing machine, was extended from the first floor, though a smaller beam, called the tron, remained at the market cross. Certain units of measurement were basic. A great pound, or clove, weighed seven pounds or half a stone. A tod was two stone, a pisa half a sack or thirteen stone. The Assizes of Weights and Measures (1171) were supposed to regularize these units, and in Norcaster all weights and measures were delivered up for inspection on the first day of the new mayoralty.

The press at the gates was greatest on market days. The four mills had been clattering since dawn when the horns sounded shrilly from the gate towers and the sergeant-at-arms lifted the heavy bars and pushed open the creaking timber gates. Carts laden with country produce lumbered through the streets toward rented stalls in the square. Outsiders leased stalls by the year and paid for the privilege through tolls called stallage. Cornmongers paid pavage for portions of pavement on which to lay their heavy sacks of grain.

Transactions were made by barter and also by money payment. The standard coin was a silver penny, twelve of which made a shilling. At one period they contained as much silver as our old dimes. The pound, not minted but used for calculations, was worth twenty shillings. A mark was figured at two-thirds of a pound; the groat, a thicker coin, was worth four times the ordinary penny. The only English gold coin was the noble, created by Edward III. Norcaster was one of the few English towns with a right to a mint, a privilege bought by the council for twenty pounds. The dies the Norcaster mint received from the Royal Exchequer showed the King's face on one side and the name of Norcaster on the other.

Large accounts were kept as written records on paper or parchment, and temporary accounts on tablets or wood coated with wax, on which the figures were etched with a bone stylus. The introduction of Arabic numerals in the twelfth century simplified computing.

For the illiterate there were two ways of keeping books. One was the counting board or exchequer, a table marked in squares on which a shopkeeper, by moving counters, could show how small and larger units added up in the cost of an item. In commoner use were the tally sticks. These were wooden paddles cut lengthwise in two sections, one given to the creditor, the other to the debtor. When partial payment was made, a notch was cut in both sections. The tallying of the two notches signified a receipt. When one person held both sections, the account was closed.

Merchants dabbled in usury, or charge for the use of money. Usury was forbidden to Christians, but when the Jews were evicted from England in 1290, the lending of money at interest continued just the same. There were ways of skirting the letter of the law, as merchants' account books show. Most of these techniques had to do with the extension of credit. The merchant would charge abnormally high prices for an item, and the buyer wasn't required to pay until later. Sometimes sharpsters created fictitious sales to conceal time loans.

The standard of living was subject to wild fluctuations—so much depended on a good harvest, and on health and peace in the land. On the average, however, a craftsman earned from four pence to eight pence a day, and a cock cost him one and a half pence, a sheep carcass a shilling. A penny would purchase ten eggs, or a gallon of ale, or two good-sized loaves of bread.

Three days a week were set aside as special market days, but in a true sense the whole town was a market. The majority of houses were shops as well, and their owners offered wares for sale from the front room. The shop front was closed by two shutters; the lower, being hinged at the bottom, could be let down like a counter, and the upper, hinged at the top, pulled up to form a penthouse, or shelter for the merchandise. Canvas hangings at the side protected the shopkeeper from wind and rain. For some, a shop-front counter did not afford enough display space, and so they built ledges from the walls of their houses.

Houses were never built in a straight line, but where the carpenter or owner chose. Business acumen had as much to do with this as fancy. The idea was to impede the traffic so the passerby would have to stop, look, and perhaps buy. The tradesman did the most he could to attract attention to his wares, hawking them in a loud voice, even dragging reluctant customers into the shop. A silent advertisement was the seven-foot pole above the first story, from which he suspended a wood or iron insignia of his calling. Houses had no numbers, so the signs served as identification as well. When one townsman asked another, "Where do you hang out?" he meant it literally.

Tradesmen of a single craft worked together in

the same area, which took its name from their occupation. Smithford Street was the home of the blacksmiths; Smithford Street was the home of the Shambles or Butcher's Row. Candlewright Street, Mill Lane, and Spicer Place are familiar names in most medieval towns. Allied crafts were neighbors, and it was not unusual for a timbermonger to share a cellar with a carpenter. The tanners and butchers, who claimed hide and carcass of a single beast, shared a section by the river. The evil smell their work produced usually relegated them to the outskirts of town.

On regular market days the activity was frantic, but every day the hurly-burly of the streets assaulted the senses. The sound of countless bells pierced through the rumbling of carts on cobblestones and the shouts of the farmer as he beat his donkey up the stone-stepped lanes. Meanwhile the death crier intoned his somber plea for prayers over the ringing anvils of the smiths. People made their way the best they could through narrow streets running with offal thrown from houses or shops, or dropped by cart beasts. As they went they skirted pigs and geese that wandered about untended. The unwary risked being treated to the entrails of an old sheep flung from Butcher's Row or a cloud of feathers from Poulterer's Lane. Some ways were well-nigh impassable.

BOOTMAKER   SCISSORS SHARPENER   TAILOR

Most streets were dark even during the day, for the overhanging stories of the houses blotted out the light. The hedge around some areas was so overgrown that one could not edge past without tearing his cloak. A timberer had left a tree trunk in one street, and in another a dead horse lay unburied. The dyers overturned their vats so regularly that Dyer's Lane was a river of colors. A rainy day was only a partial blessing; the water did wash the accumulated filth down the gutter in the center of the street, but the lack of drainage ditches meant it would back up in the low places of the town. If it weren't for the rooting hogs, and the ravens and kites that swooped

35

down periodically to snatch up the choicest garbage, the sanitation would have been a good deal worse.

There really was no such thing as keeping the streets clean. Paving was expensive, and even the larger towns did not begin to pave streets regularly until the mid-fifteenth century. Sensibly enough, when the town corporation did undertake this gigantic task, it gathered revenues from tolls on carts entering the city. The individual householder was responsible for maintaining the area outside his own door. Workers called scavagers kept pavements in repair and looked out for fire hazards. Street cleaning fell to the rakers, whose task it was to scoop the worst of the debris into a cart and haul the refuse to dumps at the outskirts of town.

The streets were not only offensive but dangerous as well. During the day a man could be run over by a cart or trampled by a horse, or just as easily killed in a brawl. Nights were more perilous still, when the only light might be the dim shine of a church altar lamp. Anyone who walked abroad had to carry a lantern or torch so he could be recognized by his neighbors. Curfew closed the taverns at nine or ten, and any stranger still within the suburbs or walls had to be answered for by his host. Nightwalkers up to no good usually wore masks.

So town and townsfolk went the daily round from

daybreak to nightfall, their work as various as they were themselves. Though there was neither Jew nor leper, every other rank or kind of man knew the town of Norcaster—the noble in his town house, a knapsacked pilgrim on his way to the Shrine of Our Lady of Walsingham, the visiting merchant with his letter of free passage, and the miserable rat-catcher.

But it was not profession so much as status that distinguished one townsman from another and the townsmen from the other subjects of the king. By the middle of the twelfth century a man could achieve free status if he had lived in a borough for a year and a day and then placed himself in scot and lot with the burgesses. This meant he had a burgage tenure or paid rent and taxes on his property. By the end of the 1300's citizenship could be obtained by birth, apprenticeship, purchase, gift, or marriage. No matter which way it was obtained, citizenship was a great personal privilege, one that marked the medieval townsman as a man apart. He was neither noble nor peasant. He owed nothing to family, class, or patron. His rank in society depended upon his success in the market. But even the least successful townsman (and there was a large percentage of un-skilled labor in every town), if he was free, found his destiny bound up with the community's.

2 Government and Guilds

Population centers today tend to resemble one another, but in medieval times, each community differed greatly. The three basic economic, political, and social units were castle, village, and town; each had a particular nature. Throughout England, but especially along the borders of Wales and Scotland, physically forbidding stone keeps surrounded by walled yards and ditches had been erected. These castles, belonging to the king or to nobles, were mainly military strongholds, harboring garrisons of fighting men and necessary provisions. The great virtues of castle life were martial ones. Young knights practiced archery and jousted in tournaments, swearing allegiance to a code of Christian gallantry, as they prepared to follow their lord in any war, public or private. The manor estates of barons or bishops were agricultural. In the south, east, and north of the kingdom the elongated S patterns of their ridged and furrowed fields radiated into the landscape. More often than not, tiny peasant villages nestled close to half-fortified stone manor houses or to chapter houses of abbeys and monasteries. At ports and along the rivers, at natural internal crossroads, stood the cities and boroughs of the land. Some towns were scarcely larger than overgrown villages; some were pretentious cathedral cities like York or bustling ports like Hastings; and some were like Norcaster, neither very large nor very small. (Only ten English towns had a population of many more than six thousand.) Towns grew naturally out of trade, as indeed trade issued from the town. English towns grew most often from a village already situated at a natural crossroads of commerce—at the ford or bridge of a river, or at that point where a river became no longer navigable inland. Here the merchant bringing goods from across the sea for sale or exchange had to shift his wares from ship to caravan.

English towns like Norcaster, with "caster" or "chester" in their names, boasted ancient origins. They were invariably Roman fortified settlements dating back as far as the first century. Sometimes urban life was engendered in walled enclosures built for defense against the Vikings in the ninth and tenth centuries. There were also many new towns, planned communities created by forward-looking nobles or kings who recognized the added value of a prosperous town in their demesne. Once established, towns often grew at the expense of a manor lord, for a knight financially ruined by the Crusades would often sell freedom to his tenants and land and privileges to a town to replenish his fortune. The king bargained in the same way, for the crown waged expensive wars. Norcaster was fortunate in being a royal borough. Towns in the king's domain had an absentee landlord, a happy contrast to a residing abbot or baron, whose interests often conflicted with those of the growing borough. Also, kings were freer in granting charters than their vassals were. Richard the Lion-hearted and John, who needed money to conduct wars abroad and repress powerful barons at home, together gave out 250 borough charters, or written documents that protected a town's customary rights and privileges.

A charter was vital to a town, for no matter how old the town, or how new, how small or how large, a town's prosperity depended on its success in commerce and its right to profit from it. Before the Conquest in 1066, some towns had established customs and enjoyed a number of privileges. These were really civic units, a group of burgesses drawn together by mutual responsibilities into a community which held regular meetings and had necessary officials for the transaction of affairs.

In the Domesday Book, a national accounting

ordered by William I in 1085, the community of Norcaster was reckoned as coextensive with the territory of a hundred. Since Anglo-Saxon times the land had been divided into administrative and judicial units called shires, hundreds, and vills, each of which had its own court. The shire territory was sometimes identical with that of the county, sometimes smaller. Its subdivision, the hundred, was an area large enough to support a hundred families, or possibly to supply a hundred fighting men to the national militia. Some boroughs were parts of hundreds, and some, like Norcaster, *were* hundreds. The vill, though it had its own market court, was more of an economic unit than a political one, and was counted as part of a hundred. In general, a king's official administered each shire and hundred; a sheriff collected revenues and presided over the shire court held twice a year, while his deputy, the bailiff, conducted the hundred court once a month.

The Domesday Book also mentions Norcaster as having a *Communis Burgensium*, a corporate society of burgesses, 276 in number, who owned 355 houses and 1,296 acres of land. As a body they held certain lands for the use of all, a pact with the king to protect their customs, and the ferm or "fee farm" of the borough for an annual rent of fifty-five pounds. "To farm" meant to collect and remit taxes. In other words, all dues owed to the lord had been commuted to a payment of a lump sum. To hold the farm of a borough and to have it collected by the town's own officials rather than by the sheriff of the county was usually the first liberty formally recognized and legalized by a charter. With it was usually granted the right to a merchant guild, giving the burgesses a monopoly of trading in their town.

Towns were not at first independent autonomous units, and they had no strong community sense. But as their prosperity grew, so did their communal spirit; the wealthiest communities were the first to purchase charters.

Norcaster was one of the few to secure a charter before the end of the twelfth century. Norman traders had established themselves there shortly after the Conquest and brought new energy into the community. In 1154 the burgesses of Norcaster approached Henry II for a charter. As the first step they swore to their ancient rights, liberties, and customs before the king's itinerant justices, who confirmed them. The agreement was then written on the patent rolls and a copy delivered into the hands of the borough to be entered in the town's White Book (its list of customs and privileges), and stored in the town's treasure box. Norcaster's first charter began like this:

Henry, king of the English and duke of the Normans and of the men of Aquitaine, count of the Angevins, to the bishops, earls, barons, justices, sheriffs, servants, and all his liegemen both French and English of Norcaster, GREETING.

Know that I have granted to my citizens of Norcaster all their liberties and customs and laws which they had in the time of Edward and William and Henry, kings of England. And I have granted them their gild merchant, with all its liberties and customs in lands and marshes, woods and pastures and other things, as well and freely as they had it in the time of our aforesaid predecessors, kings of England. And all the men who live within the four divisions of the city and attend the market shall stand in relation to gilds and customs and the assizes of the city, as well as ever they stood in the time of Edward, William, and Henry, kings of England.

Further, I have granted and confirmed to them that they shall be quit of toll and passage and of all customs throughout England and Normandy, by land and water. . . .

Special addenda to the charter pertained to the particular concerns of Norcaster: the right of working a monopoly of dyed cloth in the district (reckoned at ten leagues in every direction); the privilege of a town fishery; the power to demand a tax called murage of freemen for repair of the walls and to collect dues for river passage.

A royal writ was delivered during the same period, and it too was duly recorded in the White Book.

> Know that I [Henry II] have delivered my town of Norcaster to my burgesses at Norcaster to be held by them at "farm" from me in chief by the same "farm" which the sheriffs were wont to pay me, so that the burgesses shall henceforward answer for it at my Exchequer.

The last major privilege that Norcaster gained before the close of the thirteenth century was the right to hold two fairs, one at Whitsuntide, six weeks after Easter, and the other at the end of September, at Michaelmas.

Norcaster's charter, like other borough charters, was added to and reconfirmed at great expense under each new reign. Some important gains in later charters were the right to hold a borough court with the privilege of sac and soc and the permission to elect town officials. The court reserved all jurisdiction but the king's business, and the right of sac and soc turned the profits from transactions of internal affairs over to the town. The town's ability to choose its own magistrates also loosened the royal hold and insured extensive corporate freedom.

The town was a legal entity, a corporate being that, by dealing collectively with the lord or his agent, could act on its own to preserve its existence and further its interests. For instance, when charter rights of various towns conflicted, lawyers studied to discover which of the disputed grants was of greatest antiquity. The corporations could also make treaties for the convenience of their merchants who kept up an incessant intercourse between the towns. By the end of the fifteenth century most town corporations could possess and assign property, and even sue and be sued.

The privilege of supervising trade was unique to the medieval town, and of all the customs it claimed, the earliest and most important were a market and a merchant guild. The merchant guild was formed of all traders in a town who joined together to obtain the right to buy and sell free of tolls. Tolls or trading charges were always a burden, and exemption from them was valuable because it freed the merchants to do business in a large area. The merchant guild also formed its own market monopoly, forcing outsiders to pay tolls on goods entering the gates, rents on stalls in the marketplace, and fees for the use of the town's weights and measures. One writer has called the merchant guild a commercial club, whose members were united by a bond of fellowship in sharing advantages. The guild and its jurisdiction over trade and manufacture assured the profits of the town market for the freemen of the borough. Any "foreigner," as a non-citizen was tagged, was subjected to severe restrictions in trading and a variety of heavy market tolls.

In the thirteenth century the business of the town had grown complicated, spawning a new class of workers. During this period various individual crafts sprang up to supply the needs of the town and to export goods as well. Because each one was concerned with the production and sale of a certain article, they formed separate guilds, paying a fee to the crown for the privilege of monopoly. Every new craft that appeared sapped the strength of the merchant guild, and in the fourteenth century it disappeared altogether. Of course the richest traders of the merchant guild, the mercers, drapers, and grocers, were officers of guild and town. When they formed their own craft guilds, they retained their municipal power. It was natural that as the merchant guild faded as an economic force, its leaders should reappear in another organization associated for the particular purpose of gaining political power.

There had grown up in the town, in addition to

THE GROCER WAS A GENERALIST, WHO SOLD THE
PRODUCTS OF OTHERS.

the craft guilds, a number of religious fraternities, whose functions were, ostensibly, purely charitable and social. Again, like drew like, and guilds were formed of those with common economic interests; the mercantile traders banded together in one guild, the metalsmiths in another, the victuallers in still another, and so forth. There were over two dozen of these in Norcaster, and most of them were non-political, meeting once a year, promoting charity and good fellowship. Three of these, however, the Guild of the Holy Trinity, the Guild of St. George, and the Corpus Christi Guild, had greater ambitions than that of offering candles in chantries. They were already moneyed powers that owned several public buildings in the town when in 1381, shortly after the Peasants' Revolt, they joined forces. In one all-powerful Corpus Christi Guild, they tightened their organization and exerted even more influence over the affairs of the town.

The new guild did not itself govern Norcaster, but the twenty-four members of the town council were to a man sworn members of the Corpus Christi Guild, and as the town rolls show, the mayor of Norcaster one year often appears as guild master the next.

Meanwhile, the council took to itself the power to pass on the legality of all guild rules. Though the individual craft guilds grew in number, they remained

48

economic tools of the council. Not until the late fifteenth century did they succeed in loosening the hold of the powerful oligarchy that had its roots in the merchant guild.

By the end of the fourteenth century craft guilds represented all economic levels. Some, like the cornmongers, or dealers in grain, and the woolmen, dealt in raw stuffs locally produced. Others were importers, like the fishmongers and wine merchants, or vintners. Some traded in goods made by others; grocers and mercers sold a variety of merchandise garnered from small workshops. The clothiers were early capitalists who contracted for piecework, turning the product of many hands into a handsome profit for themselves. The average townsman worked on a particular article or articles and dealt directly with the consumer; the cordwainer made and sold shoes, and the turner, wooden measures.

But whether the guild was small and its craft undistinguished, or a large and powerful fraternity of merchants, its members' concern was the same—to reserve the fullest advantage of their trade for themselves. This they did very effectively by limiting memberships, imposing stiff admission fees, and setting conditions of manufacture and sale. They watched over their rights and reputations with jealous eyes. Each guild had its own headquarters and held meetings regularly to make rules and collect dues. Guild laws regulated internal affairs, and dealt mostly with balancing manufacture among themselves and limiting the activity of their rivals. Each craft also prohibited deceitful devices to defraud the "poor commons," as the general public was referred to, and the town council enforced craft rules.

As a trade kept to its district, so a craftsman was supposed to keep to his trade. For instance, both the cobblers and the cordwainers were leatherworkers and dealt with one product, shoes, but only the cordwainer could make new shoes—the cobbler was limited to repairing old ones. Neither one was allowed to do his own curing; that was the job of the tanners and tawyers. Often a single item of manufacture would pass through the hands of several guilds. The saddlers employed the joiners, who made the wooden framework of the saddle, the painters, who decorated it, and the lorimers, who supplied the harness and trappings. In London in 1327 there was a terrible fracas in the streets between the saddlers and the brethren of the other three guilds. The saddlers protested that their employees had organized a union to strike, and they tried to raise prices. To counter this, the other guilds charged the saddlers with conspiracy to bind their workmen to supply them only. The mayor had to call a "love-day" (a court sitting) in order to have the matter settled.

It sounds as if the guilds were at each others' throats; sometimes they were with their severest rivals, and with members who didn't conform to the rules, but they were essentially friendly societies, formed for mutual benefit. Dues went to provide for a member's burial, or help his widow, or endow a chantry priest to pray for the souls of guild members who had been too busy in their daily round to tend to spiritual matters. Guild money also fed the poor, financed such civic improvements as rebuilding a church or repairing a bridge, and supported pageants and miracle plays.

The average craft guild was divided vertically as well as horizontally, into a company of skilled and unskilled, teachers and students, employers and laborers. The wardens were official directors of activities throughout the guild; the master was the owner of his shop, the skilled workman who passed on his knowledge to apprentices, whom he trained in the trade. The journeyman was hired help, who had not yet the skill, money, or opportunity to set up his own shop. An apprentice, who had to be a freeman, was taken into the trade at thirteen or fourteen for a period of seven or more years. For a cash payment he entered into a contract with the master to learn the secrets of the trade, or mystery, as each craft was called, to be clothed, housed, and fed, and sometimes schooled, by his employer. Masters did not always keep their bargains, nor did apprentices. Some youngsters fled forever from ill use. Others ducked work for ale-drinking sprees, or an afternoon of bowling on the green. Strikes among journeymen who felt they were unfairly treated were fairly common. Rules protected both employer and employee. One poor soul apprenticed himself to an upholsterer in Cambridge who had passed himself off as a draper, and the lad didn't discover the difference for three years. When he reported the fraud to the authorities, the guild court returned him his entrance fee. The story has a happy ending; the boy found a draper to take him in, and rose to prominence in the town.

After a certain number of years, when the apprentice presented a "masterpiece" as proof of his skill to the wardens of his craft, he became a journeyman. In the first days of the craft guilds, when members of one guild were all one class, bound together by a common skill, the apprentice could have looked forward to early self-employment. To become a master at the end of the fourteenth century, however, required more than a masterpiece. One had to spend a number of years as a wage earner, being tried by a number of masters, and acquire enough money for the "upset fee," or price of setting up in business.

THE BASKET WEAVER
WAS AN INDEPENDENT
CRAFTSMAN WHO
SOLD HIS HANDI-
WORK DIRECTLY
TO THE PUBLIC.

Sometimes the only hope of advancement lay in marrying the master's daughter or widow.

There were several reasons for the change from democracy to oligarchy in guild affairs. As the nature of manufacture shifted from local retail handicraft to wholesale production of goods, friction between small craft masters and large commercial masters grew proportionately. Then too, the increased population of the town meant heightened competition within the crafts. Those lowest in the scale, the journeymen, suffered the most, for they were kept from profits or promotion. In the fifteenth century they formed their own associations, which have been called the first trade unions, because all members belonged to the wage-earning class.

The pattern of change from government by consensus to government by a few was paralleled in the town's political sphere. The story of the development of a governing body in English towns is not everywhere the same. Each town's government and institutions were influenced by previous history and modified by such local circumstances as geographical site, major resources and crafts, and the contract with the lord of the manor, be he bishop, baron, or king. The case of Norcaster was a common one. As early as the Domesday survey, we have a record of a *Communis Burgensium* in Norcaster, a corporate society of burgesses, which held certain lands in common use and had made a pact with the king to pay the customs due him. As a royal holding, Norcaster was supervised by a portreeve, but the town's civic and economic leaders were those who, in one capacity or another, made ordinances for town and market and managed the town's revenues.

For a number of years the common folk of Norcaster, called by the crier, had assembled in the
marketplace. There in the shadow of St. George's
Church, they voiced "assent and consent" to the
ordinances of the town. But as the population grew,
this method of law-making grew unwieldy, and the
majority of citizens, feeling further and further removed from the center of political life, lost interest in
forming decisions. In Norcaster, from the twelfth
century, a special jury of twelve had been chosen to
uphold the liberties of the borough. It was customary
to appoint such groups to handle special aspects of
public business. Through the years the wisdom of
having a standing body of men knowledgeable in
civic affairs, always willing and ready to judge, became apparent. At the end of the fourteenth century
only twenty-four men governed the fate of Norcaster.
These were the members of the common council, "the
most good men and the wisest of the town," chosen
"to truly help and counsel the mayor." They formed
among themselves a Board of Trade to manage inland
and foreign commerce, affairs with the king and other
boroughs, a Treasury Board to deal with revenues,
and a legal committee to handle business arising out
of these departments. As officers of the town, they
and the mayor were makers of laws and dispensers of
justice, guardians of standards in the marketplace,
and collectors of taxes, tolls, and other revenues.

Twelve of the twenty-four were in reality a permanent jury, who sat at the court leet and were elected yearly by their own number; but the other twelve were chosen by general assembly. This much of popular government the commons had saved for themselves. In former years, the mayor, too, was elected by the consent of the community; at this period in Norcaster, the twenty-four selected two men for the office, and the outgoing mayor chose between them. The mayor, of course, was the leading official of the town. A good mayor represented the town in all its affairs with the crown and with other towns of the realm, was protector of its liberties, defender in times of war, chief magistrate in the weekly borough court, and holder of the keys to its treasure. The honor of the town was his responsibility, and he was required not only to serve if summoned to office but to pay corporate debts from his own pocket, should the town fall on hard times.

By the mayor's authority the council watched over and guided the town. Four aldermen presided over the four wards of Norcaster, supervising town property and providing for miscellaneous expenses. These aldermen used to own the jurisdiction of their individual wards, paying rent for the right to administer its affairs as if it were a manor. Under them the bailiffs held the ward courts, collected taxes, and

56

were responsible for the farm of the borough. City sergeants and constables were keepers of the peace, watchers of the walls, and followed "hue and cry" (the shouts of townsmen calling attention to a crime) into the town streets to herd all evildoers into custody. The chamberlains oversaw the common pasture and put the murage money to good use, while under the vigilant eye of the town clerk the rolls of the town mounted higher and higher, bearing witness to the town's vitality. Special justices, though chosen locally, were agents of the king. They administered national legislation that was locally enforced. While the mayor supervised the view of frankpledge and lesser borough courts the justices tried cases of felony four times a year at the court leet.

Justice was only one concern of the town's administrators. Their major activity was financial. It cost a good deal of money to run a town, so the gathering of revenues was serious business. Besides the multitudinous tolls, taxes, and fines, and the revenue from markets and fairs, the town made money by conducting scot ales. For these the townsmen were obliged to provide malt for ale and then compelled to buy the brew at a fixed price. The proceeds went to the town.

Both national and municipal governments were paternalistic. The theory was that if all trades and manufactures were to be carried on for the public good, then all should be subject to public control. The wardens of each craft on taking office vowed to "consent to nothing against the state, peace, and profit of our sovereign lord king, or of the city," and no craft ordinance had force unless approved by the town council. It was considered the duty as well as the right of the corporation, and sometimes the crown, to fix prices, quality, time and place of sale, rates of wages, and hours of labor. Though the crown's attempt to regulate wages by the First Statute of Laborers in 1351 never succeeded in practice—the law of supply and demand proved too strong —a forceful royal government asserted national control over prices and quality in the most basic crafts. The Assize of Measures in 1197 and the Assize of Bread instituted in the reign of Henry II (1154–1189) were soon followed by the Assizes of Ale and Cloth. The principle behind the assizes was to assure the consumer quality in his purchase and to prevent the seller from making an excessive profit. Through the assizes the price of manufactured goods was fixed by the cost of raw material. Every year at Michaelmas, when the harvest was gathered in, the price of grain was established. Then wheat was purchased, sent to be milled, and baked into bread. The expense of milling and baking was added to the price of wheat to determine the total cost in halfpence. The dough was divided so that each loaf would be worth a halfpenny. The loaves were weighed while hot to establish the weight of a halfpenny loaf. The better the harvest, the heavier the halfpenny loaf. The price of ale was determined by the price of barley malt. The brew was supposed to cost as many farthings a gallon as malt cost shillings a quarter of a hundredweight.

Cloth was such an important export that its quality and standards of measurement were fixed by the crown. The Assize of Cloth was always conducted by a royal inspector from London, the aulnager, rather than by a local official. In general, prices for raw materials varied, and work values remained fixed. Wages in the same trade were the same for all. If one man did better work than another, then he received more work to do.

Local officials enforced such national statutes as those against the forestaller, who intercepted goods on the way to market to corner the supply or add handling charges and so force prices up. They also approved all weights and measures and saw to it that goods were sold by official standards, not by handful or by jug. Shops had to be open to the street and work done in full view. Night work was prohibited because it might be done badly and not be found out. Each craftsman was obliged to affix his own mark to his work—a mason chiseled his onto a stone, the silversmith engraved his on a silver chalice. Restrictions on the bakers were typical. They had to make loaves of two sizes, two for a penny, and four for a penny, and bake either brown bread or white, not both. They were not allowed to resell any grain they might have acquired or retail flour to a pastry cook. Each baker stamped his loaves and sold only in the marketplace, unless he had a license to employ a regrator, or middleman vendor. Naturally the corporation could not make all these rules and regulations work, but they did a creditable job by means of very thorough inspection and surveillance. Tradesmen concentrated in one area of town made the corporation's work easier, and shoddy work could be quickly traced to its source by its mark.

This obviously rigid system lent a certain amount of stability to the economic life of the town, but it was an impediment to technical progress. Many left town for rural districts to escape guild and town regulations. Then, too, as the economy became more sophisticated, industry changed from being craft dominated to a domestic system. When work was farmed out in this way, the worker lost his independence to the capitalist merchant. In Norcaster at the end of the fourteenth century only the clothworkers had stepped firmly into the new social and economic order. The rest of the individual craft guilds were enjoying a heyday.

3

Tools and Trades

THE BUILDERS AND DECORATORS

Norcaster was a town of craftsmen, artisans, and merchandisers in a variety of commodities, each busy at his special trade. The building and decorating crafts were never at a loss for work. A journeyman wanted to raise his shakily built hut, which had fallen down on Rotten Row; a fishmonger ordered a new house from the carpenter; or the Corpus Christi Guild decided to enlarge its headquarters, or endow St. George with a new fresco. When in 1387 the rebuilding of the great guildhall was begun, masons came from all parts of the country to work on the project and set up their lodge by its side.

The Masons

During the Middle Ages there were two orders of masons, the stonemasons and the freemasons. The stonemasons, sometimes called setters or layers, built the walls, and the freemasons, or hewers, worked freestone, the blocks that were separately

61

shaped or carved, like the arch moldings. The masons' guild differed from other guilds in a special way. The great centers of wealth in Europe were few, and the masons wandered from one to another wherever their work led them. They had no permanent guildhall, unlike the town guilds, and were subject to self-imposed rules. Their headquarters was a lodge, built on the site of their work, and here they ate, slept, held meetings, and elected a master and wardens to supervise them, and a clerk to keep the financial records.

The master mason was the architect, engineer, and contractor of the Middle Ages, responsible for the choice of stone, the firmness of the foundation, as well as the overall plan and artistic detail of the construction. He directed the workers and, like any guild master, was in charge of their well-being, the quality of their work, and their rate of pay.

The masons' day began at dawn and ended at sunset, with very little time off for breakfast, alebreaks called nuncheons, and dinner. Building something as ambitious as a guildhall or a church was an enormous task, for tools were few, and most work had to be done by hand. After plans and specifications had been drawn up, the masons dug a deep foundation. Then they pitched in broken stone or drove piles into the ground and covered them with flat

stones and mortar. They almost always used local stone, because the cost of carting was so high. To save another expense, the blocks were often shaped at the quarry from models in wood or canvas—an early venture in prefabrication. But this was not always the case; sometimes the masons had to cleave the stones themselves, hammering a wedge into the natural seam and splitting it with a mighty wrench of an iron crowbar. For rough hewing they used axes, and for the final dressing, a hammer and steel chisels ground to a fine edge by the blacksmith. The walls of great stone edifices were faced with finely hewn, smooth rectangular blocks called ashlar, divided by lines of flat stones known as tables. The topmost table was a corbel table, made of quaintly carved blocks that acted like brackets to support the roof timbers. All the complicated business of mullions, or vertical stone bars, for windows and springers, or bottom stones, for arches and vaulting, was built into the masonry.

The noise and activity at a building site were terrific. As the walls grew higher and higher, the masons would shout at the hod carriers and mortarmen to hurry along, and call for a rope and tackle to hoist the stone. Tables on tall trestles could be used as platforms up to twenty feet, then these were discarded for scaffolding, made of primitive rope-and-pole ladders with platforms. Hoisting machines like the crane, windlass, pulley, and lever slowly shifted stones into place.

The Carpenters

The roof and timber interior of the building was the carpenter's charge. The simplest sort of roof was constructed with rafters joined in inverted V's

CARPENTERS

and held by a ridge pole. Timber uprights secured in wall plates or tie beams supported the pole. The great invention of the carpenters of this period was the hammerbeam roof. In earlier times the tie beams stretched atop the walls, and in the center of each was a post reaching to the ridge pole. Struts or braces curved like half-moons transferred the weight from the tie beams down the wall. The glory of the hammerbeam roof was that it opened to view the beauty and height of the roof. The center of the structure was simply cut away, leaving hammerlike projections at each side, while the weight of the roof was shifted down the struts by individual posts on each projection. The exterior of the roof was nailed with laths, to wait the services of the tiler. The most beautiful and famous example of the hammerbeam roof is Westminster Hall, built in 1394, the eighteenth year of Richard II's reign, but it is said that the guildhall of Norcaster was its inspiration.

The Decorators

Naturally, the carpenter was dependent on other craftsmen; the timberer who cut in the forest, and the sawyer who squared planks from rough logs preceded him, and the slater or tiler followed him; but it was the carpenter who did the cutting and finishing and carving. We owe the intricately carved choir stalls and church screens, those marvels of the Middle Ages, to unknown artists in wood. The carpenter's common tools were the ax and broadax, adze, square, planer, and two-handed saw. The adze, a hatchet with a cutting edge fitted at right angles to the handle, was used to trim edges, as was the planer, a blade with two handles, resembling the modern drawknife or spokeshave. The carpenter made his own wooden pegs but turned to the blacksmith for his nails. Paneling and other inside work was fixed to the surface with a casein glue, soft cheese pounded with warm water in a mortar. The moisture was squeezed out and mixed with quick-

MEDIEVAL WOODWORKING TOOLS

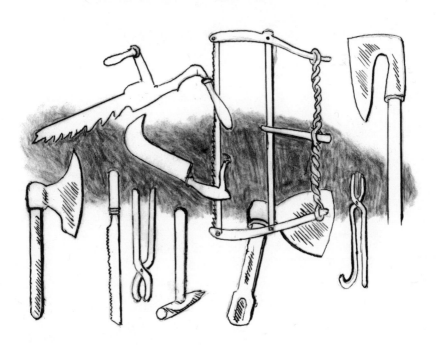

TURNER

lime. Leather was glued to wood in the same way. The tilers, painters, and glaziers illuminated the rest of the interior—tiles of geometric design in green, yellow, and red, glass panes infused with brilliant blues, greens, reds, and golds, and frescoes in fresh tempera.

Other Woodworkers

Wood was plentiful and not difficult to work, so the great number of craftsmen engaged in woodworking is not surprising. The coopers with their mauls nailed casks and tuns for everyone, not just the vintners and brewers. The turners molded wooden measures for the victuallers and bowls for the housewife, and the joiners joined pieces of wood together to make furniture. The bowyers and fletchers provided bows and arrows for the town guard. As was usual in closely related trades like woodworking and metalworking, responsibility for single articles

COOPERS

constantly overlapped. A knife in the making would pass from the bladesmith to the hafter, who fitted the handle, to the sheather, before it was finally offered for sale by the cutler. The joiner fashioned the hutches in which the burger stored his valuables, but the blacksmith attached the ornamental hinges, and the locksmith supplied the locks.

THE METALWORKERS

England was famous for its metalwork in the Middle Ages, made not only from domestic ores but also from precious imported metals. The most important metalworkers in the town were the black-smiths, who specialized in various products, ranging in size from the gargantuan bells of the founders to the tiny, odd-shaped nails of the nailmaker. Farriers shoed horses, and spurriers made spurs for horsemen. In the larger towns and cities the armorers separated into very distinct crafts: the bracers and gogarciers made armor for arms and throat, heaulmen forged helmets, bladesmen fashioned spears, swords, and daggers. By the end of the fourteenth century chain mail had been nearly replaced by plate armor, but the cardwiredrawers still made links for the town guard. Taking rods from the brakemen, the cardwiredrawers would soften the metal and draw it with pincers through progressively smaller holes until it was the

JOINER

desired thickness. Then they wrapped the metal around bars to make links. The same craft produced carding combs for the cloth industry.

Whether nailmaker or armorer, the smith followed the same pattern of work. As his apprentice blew the furnace coals bright with a bellows, the smith, wearing a bull's hide apron and leather gauntlets to protect himself from flying sparks, watched critically. Then he began to cast his crude ingots, pulling iron from the smelter pit with long-handled tongs to lay it on the anvil. From time to time, as he pounded the chunk into shape, he poked it back into the fire to

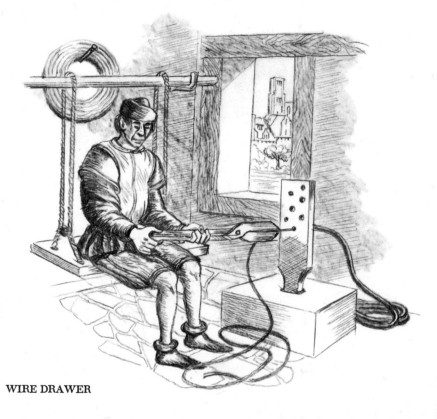

WIRE DRAWER

soften it. To temper the iron, he heated it to a glow, then sprinkled it with powdered oxhorn and salt and plunged it into water. Loud shouts and sounds resounded throughout Smithford Street. The steel hissed in a trough while the smith, his face flushed with heat, shouted to his apprentice and beat out a tatoo with his hammer. Smiths were not allowed to work at night in Norcaster, but in some place the rule must have been broken, or an anonymous poet never would have complained that

Swart [dark] smoky smiths smutted with smoke
Drive me to death with din of their dints;
Such noise at night heard no man never,
Such crying of knaves and clattering of knocks,
The pug-nosed bumpkins cry for "Coal, coal!"
And blow with their bellows till their brains are
    all bursting.

"Lus! bus! las! das!" they roar in a row,
Like a dreadful dream—may it go to the devil!

Medieval English blacksmiths did commendable work, but high art came from the potters (brass pot makers), coppersmiths, pewterers, and goldsmiths. Workers in brass, copper, and pewter made pots and basins, candlesticks, and cruets of all shapes and sizes, plain and ornamental, but the masters among them were the creators of the severely beautiful tomb

73

effigies we call monumental brasses, and of elaborate ewers in delightful animal shapes. The pewterer worked in an alloy of tin, brass, and bismuth, and his skill in this special medium ranked him next to the goldsmith in the art of metalworking.

The goldsmith's shop did not resemble that of the ordinary smith. True, he had a furnace, but it was a

POTTERS

COPPERSMITH

small one with a hole at the top, and he mixed very small amounts of his precious metal with mercury, before he stretched it into sheets and pounded it thin with a hammer. His tools were as many and fine as the blacksmith's were few and coarse—a little chisel for engraving in amber, diamond, or marble; a harness stone for testing metals; steel files and toothed saws; gold and silver wire to mend broken things; and a rabbit's foot to make the metal gleam. His apprentice sat at a waxed table covered wih clay, care-

fully tracing designs, which he would transfer to the metal with chalk. All about the shop were examples of the goldsmith's art, crystal and gold reliquaries for the church and jeweled brooches for the mayor and his wife. The rich of Norcaster flocked to the gold-smiths with their extra money to have it made into gold plate, jewelry, and fancy girdles. A prosperous

76

guild would commission an amethyst-studded chalice for their chantry priest or a tooled silver saltcellar for guild feasts. In all of England, and on the Continent as well, it was joy and a privilege to own an object of "the touch of Norcaster."

THE LEATHERWORKERS

The leatherworkers almost equaled the metalworkers in number. These craftsmen (who bought from the skinners, who bought from the butchers) were divided into two distinct callings, those who worked the rawhides into leather, and those who turned the leather into objects for sale. The leatherdressers were the tanners, tawyers, and curriers, and true to medieval guild custom, their duties were mutually restricted. The tanners dealt with ox, cow, and calf, immersing the hides in huge vats filled with oak bark. The tawyers were limited to sheep, deer, and horse hides, which they tawed with alum and oil after the old Roman method. The curriers dressed the cured skins with tallow to make them smooth and supple. The tanner first soaked the rawhides in lime to remove the hair, then rinsed them and put in the vat with tan turves (pieces of oak bark), where they remained for a year. When properly tanned or tawed, cured, and perhaps dyed by the dyer, the leather found its way to the cordwainer, who stretched it on his last and with awl and thread stitched it into pairs of heelless slipper-shoes for the townsmen. The cordwainer was always at odds with the cobbler, who was forced to work with bazan, or inferior sheepskin, and supposed to be confined to mending old shoes. The saddlers were the other important users of tanned leather. Tawed leather was soft and spongy, especially if treated with oil, and well suited to the needs of the glovers, pursemakers, girdlers, bottlemakers, and pointmakers, who supplied the laces used to fasten cloaks and armor.

THE CLOTHWORKERS

On the downs and in the wolds and on the sloping flanks of the mountains in the west and north, thousands of sheep grazed on lands belonging to king, baron, bishop, and yeoman farmer. Since the eleventh century wool had been shipped across the Channel and North Sea to the waiting looms of the clothmakers of Flanders. But in the fourteenth century, when the Lowlands seethed with factional warfare, England, aided by the crown, began to compete seriously for the lead in European cloth manufacture. Domestic cloth industry had been active since the twelfth century, but in 1331 Edward III encouraged

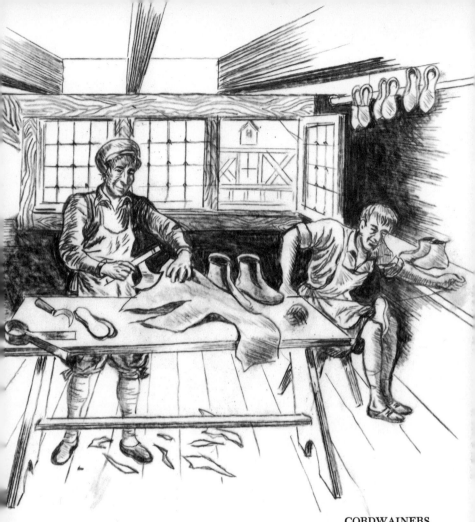

CORDWAINERS

Flemish weavers and other artisans to settle in English towns to teach his people their skills. His predecessor, Edward II, had already forbidden the import of cloth and had extended special trading privileges to the merchants of manufactured cloth. Formally restricted to producing cloth of a certain size, they were allowed to make cloth to any length or measure. In 1363 Edward III withdrew the Staple or export market for wool and cloth from Bruges and established it in the English part of Calais. Wool was still exported in volume (30,000 sacks of 364 pounds each in the fourteenth century), but the heavy tax on its export and the quasi-monopoly of the wool trade in the hands of the Merchants of the Staple spurred on the cloth industry. Along with the bales of wool, there now poured into the Staple thousands of lengths of worsted, fustian, serge, and two dozen other weaves from the towns of England. By 1400 the export of cloth had increased tenfold.

The development of the cloth manufacturing trade in Norcaster was typical. As in other towns, it was the prime force in displacing the old merchant guild and bringing the individual craft guilds into their own, for the weavers were usually the first to set up a rival organization. The trade also brought the clothiers unheard-of power and wealth. Because cloth manufacture was so complex, and because so many distinct skills were needed along the way, it was convenient for a single merchant to provide the wool and organize the manufacture step by step, paying each craftsman for his work by the piece. The clothier, as this merchant was called, was one of the first capitalists. He bought raw material and sold a finished product, investing his profits in a new cycle. His advantage lay in keeping the lesser craftsmen, especially the weavers and fullers, who washed and shrank the cloth, under his thumb. In Norcaster, even when the fulling industry moved out into the countryside where running water was plentiful to run fulling mills, the merchants retained control of the final product.

To transform a bale of oily fleece into finely woven cloth was basically the same process then as it is now. The raw wool supplied and sorted by the woolman or fellmonger had to be scoured to remove the oil and dirt before it was fluffed by the teaser. The carder, working with a flat, square paddle fixed with barbed pins of steel, aligned strands for spinning. Carding long wool was arduous work, for large combs had to be heated in open charcoal fires, and the wool pulled carefully from one to the other so no fibers broke. Many of the preliminary processes in cloth manufacture were in the hands of women. To spin by hand, the spinster (a word never applied to a man) gathered up a layer of wool into a soft roll called a rolag and wrapped it around a long stick or distaff. Holding the distaff under her left arm, she drew with finger and thumb a loosely

twisted length of wool known as a roving and fastened the end of it into a notched, tapered stick, the
spindle. A quick twist of the spindle, a hold, followed
by a sudden releasing movement, spun the roving
into strong thread. The spinning wheel, invented in
the thirteenth century, was in fairly common use by
the end of the fourteenth.

The spun wool then went to the weavers, already sitting at their looms, sometimes two abreast, feet on treadles, ready to weave thread into cloth. In weaving, strands of yarn are laced together and pushed tight to make one piece. The threads that run longitudinally between two rollers on the loom are called the warp, and those that run horizontally, the woof. The medieval loom was a rectangular frame, and from its corners, posts rose to form another frame above the loom. The upper frame held the pulleys over which passed thongs connected to the treadles. The loom was set up with loops of thread held at a particular distance from each other by pegs or wire teeth set into a wooden baton called a raddle and attached in alternate series to strips of wood. The heddles, as the strips are called, were lifted in turn by the treadles, so the shuttles or bobbins wound with thread could pass between, carrying the woof thread across the warp. As the shuttle flew back and forth, the weaver, with his free arm, pushed the batten, a vertical frame of rods, against the crossed threads and wound the woven cloth on his roller.

Looms could be no wider than a man's reach, so the usual cloth was narrow, only one and three-quarters yards after shrinking. Two men at a wider loom could produce broadcloth. The weaving also has a great deal to do with the kind of material that is produced. Cloth can be made heavier by using more skeins in the warp or by twisting the warp thread. Serge was made with this extra twist. Districts in England were known for the kind of cloth they produced. Kersey came from Kersey in Suffolk, cheap burel from Cornwall, and worsted—from Worsted. Norcaster was celebrated for small loom coverlets and thick woolen hangings made from the middle-grade wool that Norfolk sheep bore.

Even after the weaving, there were many more things to do, as these lines from *Piers Plowman* recount:

> Cloth that cometh from the weaving is not comely to wear
> Till it be fulled under foot or in fulling stocks,
> Washen well with water, and with teasels cratched,
> Towked and teynted and under tailor's hands.

The object of fulling was to clean the raw cloth, shrink and thicken it so the weave could not be distinguished. "Fulling under foot" was the primitive method. The fuller would put cloth in his trough with water and fuller's earth (hydrous silicate of alumina), which not only cleansed the fabric, but also gave it body and helped it absorb the dye. The town fuller always trod the cloth underfoot, but in the fourteenth century, fulling stocks or mills captured the trade. By substituting two relentless, water-power-driven hammers for the aching feet of the town fuller, they left him with only caps and hures (shaggy felt hats) to keep him busy. Short wool was always fulled, but long wool used for lighter worsteds and serges usually was not. After the fulling, the fabric was stretched on a tenter, or wooden frame, to dry.

At the dyer's near the river were a number of stout vats in which he mixed his dyes with water and heated them over a fire. Sometimes cloth was dyed in the wool, but more often the dyer stirred the cloth around in his vats with a long stout staff until it reached the desired hue. His common dyes were woad for blue, madder for tomato reds and russets, and graine, to make scarlet. Weld or saffron yielded strong yellow, and lichen and other vegetable dyes produced subdued greens, yellows, and browns. Brazil, or logwood, vermilions, and graine (made from a species of Mediterranean insect) all were imported from the Venetian traders, along with a quantity of woad to supplement the local supply. The woad came in balls, which were broken and mixed with water, then allowed to ferment, being turned several times. All dyes were tempered with wood ashes or potash and mixed by a mordant or fixative

DYER

like alum, verdigris, or copperas. Like all colorists,
the dyers experimented with the primary hues to produce secondary ones, and also tried double dyeing for
special effects. Color was so important to the manufacture of cloth that many fabrics came to be called
by their hues: bluet, russet, blanchet (white), mur-
ray (orange), rosette, green, and scarlet of Lincoln.
Motley was parti-colored cloth.

86

Once tinted, the cloth went to the stretcher, who pulled it to proper size on a rack and then sent it to the rower, who pulled up the nap with teazles, or dried heads of "fuller's thistle." The shearmen snipped the loose threads and the drawer repaired any damage the shearman might have done. Then the cloth was gathered by the clothier into the searching house to be inspected for length and quality by the aulnager, the royal inspector, and sealed. From the clothier, draper, and mercer in England or abroad, it finally passed "under tailor's hands."

The tailor was a busy fellow, although he only worked for the well-to-do. Inventories of the wardrobes of the wealthy reveal an amazing number of garments. The burgher owned far more clothes than utensils or furniture. For burgher or baron, extravagant apparel, finely embroidered and lined with expensive furs, was an accepted way to display one's wealth.

THE MERCHANDISERS

The economic structure of any town shifted in ever changing patterns, but in general the chief men of merchandise were fishmongers and grainmongers, drapers or clothiers, mercers or haberdashers, who dealt in small wares, and the grocers who stocked spices. Cloth merchant, food merchant, whatever, the real moneymakers were those who lived by trade, who bought wholesale and sold retail. While the draper, under the watchful eye of the guild wardens, sold his cloths open for the customer to measure, the mercer hopped like a sparrowhawk among his assorted wares. Pins and needles, caps and boots and leather laces, whipcord and cradlebows, purses, paper, parchment and pencase, beads of alabaster and jet, crucifix and statue of St. John, spurs, eyeglasses, gaming tables, and boxes, boxes, boxes, could be found in the town mercerie. The grocer, whose name marks him as a seller in gross, stocked drugs, like an apothecary, and his trade was often subdivided into specialties of spicer, salterer, and pepperer.

THE VICTUALLERS

If cloth was the lifeblood of the country, food was its greatest necessity, and agriculture the mainstay of the domestic medieval economy. The success of his harvest and the health of his beasts meant feast or famine to the peasant and to the poorer townsman as well. The victuallers of Norcaster were members of powerful crafts—the bakers, brewers, butchers, and the cornmongers (or dealers in grain) and fishmongers. The bakers and fishmongers hired regrators, middleman vendors who hawked from door to door, mingling their cries with the street sellers of ripe strawberries and apples.

The Butchers

Almost every dish at a well-to-do burgher's table contained meat of some form, at least on days of no fast or abstinence, but it was rarely fresh. Beasts were reserved for breeding, but the majority could not be fed during the winter months. Cattle not needed for plowing were butchered after they had fattened up somewhat on the long stubble left in the reaped field; sheep not fit to bear good fleece were slaughtered next, when the mountain pastures grew thin; the hogs were killed last of all, because they could fend for themselves in the forest on acorns and beech mast. The great day of slaughter was Martinmas (November 11) and that day the Flesh-Shambles ran with blood. The meat the butchers offered, even when fresh, was hardly succulent, for it was never aged properly. Even the hogs had razor backs, and some persons swore they would rather eat the hide than the cow. Meat came into the market on the hoof, was killed and cleaned in the streets. The hides, as we have noted, went to the tawyers and tanners, and the beef, mutton, or pork was sold whole. Usually just enough meat was killed as could be sold in a day, but the butcher did his own salting, and offered cured meat to his customers. In Norcaster, as in other towns, the Flesh-Shambles was the evilest smelling quarter in town, and by ordinance was moved to the outskirts.

The Fishmongers and Cornmongers

By church decree the vigils of holydays, certain days called ember days, and all the days of Lent were meatless. This meant a bonanza for the fishmongers. Fortunately for the English, their island was rich in watery resources. The sea delivered up a bounty on all sides. Billions of herring swam from the Shetland Islands to Yarmouth in the fall. Yarmouth was the great port of East Anglia, where the herrings were salted, barreled, and sent downriver to all parts of England as well as overseas. Hake, haddock, and salmon were fished in northern waters, ling and other varieties of cod out of Scarborough and Grimsby. Whiting and plaice came from Rye and Winchester, mullet from Devon, and from all parts, dogfish, mackerel, pitchard, barbel, bream, perch, and grayling. The most plentiful shellfish were oysters and mussels. Such odd fish as porpoise and whale were considered a great delicacy, fit for a noble household. The rivers of England were not polluted as they are now, although in a sorry plight near the towns, and they supplied freshwater trout, eel, carp, and tench. Weirs and sieves were employed in river fishing; stakenets stretched twenty-four feet across the river bed; and eels were caught in bottle-shaped traps of wickerwork.

The fishmongers and the stockfishmongers, who dealt in slit, sun-dried fish, mostly cod, sold to the fishvendors, who touted their smelly goods from fishboards in the marketplace or from baskets they carted around the streets. Fish were sold in large quantities, in bushel baskets, in fact, which were supposed to hold only one kind of fish. The corn-mongers in most river or port towns were in league with the fishmongers, because the latter owned ships, and the sellers of raw grain needed convenient transport for their bulky raw produce. Another source of the cornmongers' power was their control of the mills, which they leased to millers, as the latter leased shops to bakers.

The Bakers

Bread was a staple of the diet. Every man, woman, and child ate an average of twelve pounds a week, and their appetites must have kept the baker's shovel arm very active. The town bakers made three basic kinds of bread: manchet, or simnel, was the

finest bread made from wheaten flour; the cheat-loaves were seconds; and ravel bread was made from unbolted flour mixed with the cheaper grains, bar-ley, bran, millet, rye, or oats. The loaves were kneaded into many different shapes, too, sometimes in balls and sometimes in long, thin rods. The standard loaf always sold for a halfpenny, its weight determined by the local Assize of Bread.

The Brewers

Ale was the most popular drink of the Middle Ages; the average man's consumption has been figured at a gallon a day. If he drank second-quality brew, his thirst cost him a penny. Brewing, like other home industries that did not require great strength, was a woman's job. Betty the Brewster made her ale with barley malt. (Hops were used very sparingly in the fourteenth century; the first mention of "hoppynge beer" is recorded in 1391 in London, and there was no Assize of Beer until 1441.) When the alewife had a new batch of brew for sale, she put out an alestake, or pole with a bush on the end, and called in the ale conner, or taster. For every ward in Norcaster an ale conner was appointed to set a price on ale in relation to its quality, which, according to contemporary reports, must have varied considerably. It could be as thin as barley water or so thick it looked "as if pigs had wrestled in it." By ordinance ale had to be sold in standard measures (gallon, pottle, third, and quart), but this rule, like many others, was constantly broken.

The Tavern and Cookshop

The ale conner also tasted at the tavern, the roistering public house of the town, which sold home-brewed ale, but especially wine, bought at retail from the vintners. Wines of Gascony and the Rhine were dear enough, but the very popular sweet wines, Vernage, Romney, and Malvoisie, went for as much as thirty-two pence a gallon when poured by the taverner, a price representing a week's wages for many laborers. By law, wine for sale had to be on view, usually in casks on low wooden racks, so the taverner could not mix dry and sweet on the sly. At cookshops close by, townsmen could buy roast meat of all kinds or supply the meat themselves and have it cooked for a fee.

> Cooks and their men were crying, "Pies hot, all hot,
> Good pork and good goose, come, come dine."
> Taverners told the same tale, "A drink of wine for nothing,
> White wine, red wine, to wash the roast down."
> —*Piers Plowman*

The tavern opened onto the street like any other shop, but inside a different scene tumbled into view. This was a place for idlers, gossips, gamblers, and loose women, dicing and drinking on barren oak tables. Drunken quarrels, obscene jokes, and shouted profanities drowned out the music of the minstrels who played for pence from bystanders. Gambling

94

was encouraged by the taverner, because it brought him customers and an added source of income as a pawnbroker. Of the many different gambling games, usually played with three dice, the simplest was hazard, a game rightly named. The gambler carried hope in his hand and his money in a jug, both of which were soon emptied. Some foolish persons played for all they owned, even gambling their clothes away, to stumble home in a borrowed cloak.

TRICKS OF THE TRADE

The desire to get the better of one's fellows is deeply imbedded in human nature, and swindlers were no worse in medieval days than now. Obviously, however, the number and strictness of the council and craft guild rules challenged many to outwit them. Fellmongers mixed hair with wool, and drapers and mercers stretched lengths of cloth as far as they would go, or joined a bad piece of fabric with a good one and folded it cunningly or sold it in dark corners to hide the defects. The cooks substituted rabbit for venison in their pasties, or worse, used meat from sheep that had died of plague. A baker would over-yeast his dough and sell the poor public air for bread, or hide a piece of iron in the dough to make less weigh more. The grocer moistened spices to make them heavier and sold them by the horn or hand, instead of by standard measure. One alewife put an inch and a half of pitch in the bottom of her quart measure and slyly sprinkled it with rosemary to disguise the tarry smell. Cordwainers made shoes from sheepskin instead of calf leather. Shopkeepers were not the only ones who cheated. Stonemasons or turners who worked by the day stood idle or slowed their work, and carpenters or blacksmiths who worked by the project or piece didn't spend enough time to insure quality work. A collapsed house, crooked iron hinge, or pot that melted on the fire were frauds of the same ilk. Every town had its false pilgrims and fraudulent beggars, quacks and necromancers, and swindlers of all kinds were quickly punished when caught.

Records show the most penalties for offenders against the social code, for lies uttered against the mayor or aldermen, for practicing the art of magic, pretending to be a tax collector, "exhibiting divers counterfeit bulls from the pope," like Chaucer's pardoner, for using counterfeit dice or committing a breach of chastity, as did the aptly named Miss Joan Jolybody of Norcaster. The punishment for breaking guild rules was a fine, and for repeated offenses, time in the stocks, pillory, or on the cucking stool. The stocks consisted of two beams laid

one on top of another with holes for its victim's
feet. The pillory, a more severe punishment, was
formed of a wooden frame raised on a broad platform where the prisoner stood, his head and hands
thrust through holes in the frame. A thewe was a
pillory especially designed for women, and it was
probably a thewe to which the cheating alewife
was consigned. The means of punishment were
always in full view, for part of the penance was

STOCKS AND PILLORY

public shame and exposure. If his offense was exceptionally serious, the culprit might be bound bareheaded and barefooted to a cucking stool at his own door or hauled through the street in a cart. Pipe and tabor announced the penal tumbril and townsmen stopped to hoot and jeer their unlucky neighbor. The mark of his deed was always about the offender. When a tradesman fooled the public the means of deceit was hung around his neck (a whetstone if he were a liar), while the merchandise was burned under his nose.

The shadow of the gallows fell over the grave felonies of theft and manslaughter. Grand theft was adjudged a more heinous crime than murder, because a thief could literally undo a man by seizing all his floating capital at once. Manslaughter was common for ale was cheap, tempers short, and weapons always at hand. Blows were everyday currency, and brawls could break out over nothing, leaving dead men in the streets. Every citizen was supposed to follow a hue and cry into the street and deliver wrongdoers into justice. When such a chase was on, the only chance for mercy lay in the church, where a criminal could flee for sanctuary. Once a man crossed the threshold, he was safe. The council would then call for the coroner, while the felon confessed his crimes in front of witnesses. Meanwhile, all was taken down in writing by the court clerk. The murderer's sentence was usually to "abjure the realm." Clad in nothing but shirt and breeches, he had to make his way to a port within a specified period, forty days to six months, and exile himself forever. Another way out was to claim "benefit of clergy." If a man could prove he was a cleric, or sometimes, even if he could read like one, he was remanded to the ecclesiastical court for custody, where he could not be punished for his first capital offense.

This was neither the first nor last time privilege availed a man better than he merited. The crown was unable to check the evil of maintenance, patronage of powerful barons who used bribes and threats to win judicial favor for their retainers. The borough courts, too, were rife with abuse. Every era has voiced the same complaint—wealth can buy men's souls. In the fourteenth century John Gower, in *Mirour de L'omme*, complained:

> The law is double-faced, therefore
> All justice now has lost its way
> And righteousness is gone astray.

If justice served both rich and poor, it treated the rich better.

The Professions

4

The professional men of the Middle Ages were the clergy, the lawyers, and the doctors. The clergy were numerous, and as ministers of the Church, their influence was great. The lawyers and doctors were few in number, but their professions, too, touched one and all.

THE LAW

Three main bodies of law operated in England at the end of the fourteenth century—canon law, or the law of the Church, feudal law, or the law of the manor, and common law, tempered by equity, on which royal justice was based.

The Roman Catholic Church was a separate power in the land, a power both temporal and spiritual. The foundation of the Church's strength was its dominion of fear and hope over men's souls. Life with all its miseries was but a passing phase in a timeless eternity. The Church had the keys to Paradise. By her teaching, through her grace-giving sacraments and liturgy, she could lead men to triumph over evil. To disregard her was to incur the wrath of God and to suffer forever the pains of hell.

The Church's temporal domain was also great. During the centuries it had gathered enormous wealth, by land purchase and reclamation, through acceptance of gifts and bequests, and through exactions of taxes, fines, and the fees of its courts, which had jurisdiction over a multitude of human affairs. This wealth was almost inalienable. The Church also had privileges, laws, and an organization all its own. A hierarchy encompassed every member of the regular and secular clergy from the lowest church janitor to the pope, the universal head of the Church. As a separate political power the Church was in competition with national governments for the loyalties of men and the revenues of kingdoms.

She laid claim to a field of jurisdiction wider than that of any civil code. At first she controlled not only all matters related to Church beliefs, organization, operations, and property but also those concerning morals. Her domain included laws of marriage, dowries, wills, widows and orphans, and oaths (which sealed most agreements). She demanded that all members of the clergy be tried in her courts. Besides such regular clergy as monks and friars, and the major orders of the secular clergy, bishops, priests, deacons, and subdeacons, the medieval clergy comprised staff underlings of every ecclesiastical institution, and all students and teachers at the universities. The canon law, by which the Church ruled this vast prerogative, was made of custom, writings of the Church fathers, and decisions of the popes and councils called by the bishops. It meted out punishment both physical and spiritual. Although ecclesiastical courts could not condemn a man to death, they could, through excommunication, deprive him of life in the Church.

While canon law was based on the Roman legal system, feudal law drew on Anglo-Saxon and Norman legacies. Its civil code was essentially concerned with land holdings. Since land was the chief form of wealth, it was the major cause for dispute.

When William the Norman conquered England, he granted a number of feudal rights to each vassal. Among these were the right to trial in a private feudal court and jurisdiction over his own manor. Manorial courts met several times a year to conduct such village affairs as electing a reeve, deciding petty arguments, and trying and punishing infringements of rules. By the fourteenth century the manorial courts had separated into three distinct bodies: the court customary, which tried civil suits of the serfs; the court baron, which heard civil suits of free tenants; and the court leet, whose domain was crime.

Feudal law called for judgment by one's peers. Just as nobles judged nobles in feudal courts, the members of the community testified about their neighbors in manor courts. The villagers were usually divided into groups of ten or tithings. Each man in a tithing was responsible for the behavior of his fellows, and one of their numbers, who was a tithing man, or capital pledge, was obliged to report the misdoings of anyone in his group. This system of self-policing was called frankpledge, and the local court, the view of frankpledge. It was in commonest use on manors in the south and east, which bound many serfs to the land, rather than in the Danelaw, which elected a primitive jury of freemen. Even so, as late as 1473, the town of Lynn still held a view of frankpledge, the privilege of which was the subject of hot dispute between mayor and bishop.

The law that operated in feudal courts was the law of custom, and legal procedure followed primitive codes. Private revenge was translated into public punishment, as severe fines, mutilation, branding, and maiming were meted out to the unfortunate. In an appeal to divine authority, trial by ordeal put the accused through tortures of fire or water in which only those who were not seriously injured were adjudged blameless. In some communities, drowning was considered a sign of innocence! In trial by battle, introduced by the Normans, might determined right. Trial by compurgation was less barbaric. If the evidence wasn't overpoweringly against him, the defendant could be cleared by the oaths of those who swore to his innocence. Fortunately, this less-than-equitable justice could be outlawed by communal legislation, as indeed it was in Norcaster in 1189.

Despite such divided jurisdiction, the law of the realm developed rapidly from the time of William I. During the reign of Henry II (1133–1189) royal justice provided a law common to all. Secular government had grown stronger and taken over authority in one area after another, robbing jurisdiction from feudal and ecclesiastical courts. Feudal law believed all law already existed and remained only to be interpreted, but royal government was actually making a law based on court decisions. Justice was being formed not only through custom but also through demands for action.

England had always been ruled by kings with the aid of bodies of advisers. The Anglo-Saxons had their Witangemot, or Assembly of Wise Men, and the Normans their Curia Regis, or Council of the King. At the time of the Norman Conquest William I had taken lands from the English Saxon lords and given them to his retainers in return for certain services. Thus the king became a feudal overlord with a feudal vassalage. His Council was a feudal body made up of nobles, bishops, and royal household officials.

The Council performed all three functions of government—executive, legislative, and judicial—but by the end of the fourteenth century it had divided into many branches to deal with the increasing complexity of the realm's business. Three courts of law had evolved from the old Curia Regis. The first was the Court of Common Pleas, which heard civil suits; the second, the Court of the King's Bench, which tried criminal cases; and the third, the Exchequer, which handled revenues. Officials from the courts traveled throughout the countryside to bring royal justice to the subjects of the king.

Besides the three great central courts that grew out of the Curia Regis, there also emerged the Court of Chancery. Chancery dealt in civil disputes not covered by the common law. The kind of justice it provided was called equity, because by judging each case on its own merits it promised a more equitable decision than the inflexible common law.

The parent Curia Regis, still an important judicial court, had increased its advisory capacity and came to be called the King's Council. It continued to carry out all functions of government, but when it met on judicial business it was called Parliament. The word *parliament* means discussion group, a good description of the assembly that advised, and sometimes criticized, the king. Long before Edward I (1272–1307), English kings looked to this court as a source of public opinion, but Edward I made Parliament a clearing ground for airing grievances, so it would grant him financial and military aid when he needed it. Parliament became the place where the subjects of the king could request redress of wrongs and look for action to be taken on their petitions. The Parliament traded money for concessions, such as better regional justice, and in time no important action was ever attempted, and in particular, no taxes ever levied, without Parliament's consent.

As it won a firmer hold of the purse strings, especially by the Confirmation of the Charters of 1297, by which common consent was required to exact any extraordinary financial contributions, Parliament increased its bargaining power, actually initiating legislation. If the king granted a parliamentary request, it would appear on the statute of that meeting of Parliament, and thus become the law of the land.

At the same time Parliament was becoming a representative body. The barons, earls, and bishops used to be the sole spokesmen for the realm, but during the thirteenth century the increasingly influential middle class, knights from the country and burgesses from the towns, were called separately to grant aids and to give advice to the king; the year 1295 saw a common assembly of high and low. At first the petitions of rural or urban middle class were presented independently. Then the two groups found that by joining in common petitions they had even greater power to enact law. Parliament, taking advantage of the preoccupation of Edward III (1312–1377) with the wars in France, divided itself into interest groups of "commons" and "lords" and pursued legislation with even greater fervor. At the same time, the King's Council began to specialize in judicial functions. By 1414 no law was valid unless Parliament had given its consent. Richard II, Henry IV, and Henry V, who reigned from 1377–1417, were neither absolute nor constitutional monarchs, but they were all subject to the law of the land; and it can be truly said that Henry IV was king not only by the Grace of God, but also by an Act of Parliament.

How the royal justice of the central courts was brought to the English people and how, at the same time, a uniform and rational law was formed is a story unique in the annals of jurisprudence.

107

Lawlessness always abounded in the land, but in the twelfth and thirteenth centuries nobody had the regular duty of detaining lawbreakers, accusing and prosecuting them. Villagers and townsmen alike were supposed to raise the "hue and cry" by calling after miscreants and rousing their neighbors to follow in hot pursuit. But if a criminal weren't caught red-handed or run down by some relative of the victim, he often went scot free. Local constables were appointed, but they had not enough authority to become effective keepers of the peace. The institution of special justices in the fourteenth century seemed to provide an answer. These justices, as agents of the king, were allowed to receive indictments against criminals and deliver them to the itinerant justices, the members of the Curia Regis on circuit. By written authority they were given the right to try disturbers of the peace and to hear all cases specified in their commissions. From 1388 these justices heard and judged felonies in sessions held four times a year. In effect, the old shire courts, which had been carrying on under the sharp eyes of the itinerant justices, were transferred to the authority of the bailiffs of the criminal courts, or leets.

One reason that the royal courts gained so much authority is that they offered a more equitable justice through trial by jury. The foundation of the jury system was very old. The Normans, having borrowed it from the Romans, imported the Frankish system of *inquisitio* or judicial investigation by a *jurata* or sworn group from the community. The Vikings brought the same practice to the Danelaw years earlier, but it was not until the time of Henry II that trial by jury was established as an ordinary procedure in the realm.

Two legal actions instituted by Henry II were of paramount importance in the development of the judicial system. One, called the Great Assize, declared that no free landholder could be sued concerning his land except in the king's courts. The other, known as the Assizes of Clarendon (1166), provided for a jury of the men of the district. When the king's traveling justices came to each shire, they gathered twelve men from every hundred, and four from every vill to give information under oath. In civil cases these men presented knowledge of the dispute (usually over possession of land), and in criminal cases they handed in the names of those suspected of serious crimes.

The presentments of the jury were really indictments, because the accused went directly to trial. In the fourteenth century the criminal courts, like the civil courts earlier, offered "recognition"; that is, the judge would call for a number of men, usually twelve,

109

to inquire into the case and deliver a verdict. Jury duty was a public service, and a rather unpopular one. Most jurors were exceedingly cautious because to bring in an unjust decision could result in a severe fine for them.

The devices the king used to make it possible for his subjects to partake in royal justice actually created law. We have already seen how parliamentary statutes were made into law (these were written laws, the proceedings of one session recorded and consented to by king and Parliament). The assizes were crown edicts issued as instructions to royal judges with the consent of the Great Council. Legal actions under such rules were also referred to as assizes. The writs were the real "lawmakers" of the period. An individual needed a writ to get his case heard in the king's court. Writs were written documents prescribing specific forms of judicial action. If a man had a suit that conformed to a certain writ, he could obtain the appropriate document for a fee. By calling for the application of the assizes of the king, the writs established a uniform law for similar cases.

While law was being formed in the courts of the king, lawyers were cementing it by recording court proceedings. The work of many was synthesized by one man—Henry de Bracton, who compiled *On the Laws and Customs of England* in 1250–1256. The

110

men of law, like other groups with common interests, formed associations. The most famous medieval guild of lawyers established the Inns of Court in London, converting town houses into miniature universities where civil law was taught. The Inns of Court were exclusive clubs; the masters and apprentices had the sole right of pleading in the London courts. Surely the medieval lawyers were as busy as our modern ones, dealing with disputes between citizen and citizen, town and town, as well as between borough and lord and Church and State.

MEDICINE

Medieval man was able in his practice of law, but the plight of medicine was deplorable. The lore of the doctors was a jumble of scientific truths and fables, and they had no capacity to judge between them. Medical textbooks were not lacking. From 1150 on, English scholars translated Latin versions of Greek and Arab medical works, especially by Galen and Avicenna, and other scientific treatises were available to the learned. Medical schools at Salerno and Bologna were world famous, and through practice doctors and surgeons had acquired certain skills; but from the year A.D. 200 to the beginning of the sixteenth century no real progress was made. There were several reasons for this. For one thing the

111

medieval man's inaccurate idea of the universe profoundly influenced medical theory. He believed that the earth was the center of the world, and that it stood still while the sun and moon and all the planets circled around it in nine concentric spheres, the outermost sphere separating God the spirit from his material works. The stars were fixed to the firmament, but the movements of the planets were erratic. All matter was thought to consist of four elements, earth, air, fire, and water, and these were mixed in man with an incorruptible element, his Godlike soul. In the planets, as in all matter, certain elements and "minerals" predominated, and these could be absorbed by man, influencing his health and fate. Since the unpredictable movements of planets were supposed to explain unforeseen events in the lives of men, astrology was considered an important science.

DISLOCATED SHOULDER

DISLOCATED ELBOW

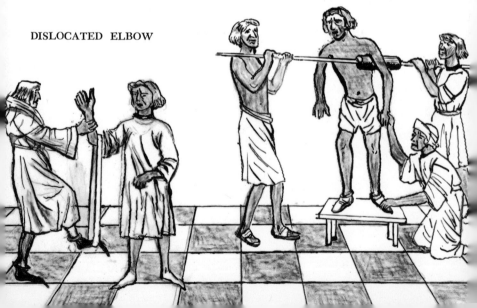

The planets' swerves were usually thought to have an unhealthy effect, but sickness was to be expected, considering the generally pernicious living standards that always preyed on the health of the people. A diet of meat and pastries encouraged disorders of the stomach, skin diseases, and tooth decay, and the crowded and unsanitary conditions of the town fanned virulent bubonic and pneumonic plagues, and epidemics of diptheria, typhus, cholera, and influenza. Leprosy was a scourge, and cancer, tuberculosis, and a host of other diseases took their toll. Sometimes an entire town would be poisoned by ergot fungus in rye. St. Anthony's fire, as this disaster was called, both tortured and disfigured its victims. The average lifespan was short, according to our standards. Only a hardy child lived to twenty. If he did, he might be expected to live a good deal longer, but he owed his fortune to a strong constitution rather than to medical expertise.

In theory the road to health was to keep the body's humors or liquids in balance. These humors were four: blood, phlegm, yellow bile, and black bile, corresponding to the principal temperaments and elements in man. Their properties, paralleling those of the four elements of earth, water, fire, and air, were hot and moist, cold and moist, hot and dry, and cold and dry. For instance, melancholy (a common com-

113

plaint) was supposed to stem from an excess of black bile, and wormwood, being "hot and moist," was prescribed to bring the humors back into equilibrium. This sort of diagnosis was properly the realm of the physician, or doctor of physic, the first of three orders of medieval medical man. The physician, who ranked over the master surgeon and barber surgeon, kept a supply of drugs and ointments from the apothecary. A scholar, he was the internist of the Middle Ages; that is, he made the diagnoses. His few methods of examining the patient were elementary: looking at the tongue and urine, and taking the pulse. Plasters and poultices, hot bricks, lancets, drains, dilator, and dysterpipe were part of his equipment for treating fevers, abcesses, and skin diseases.

Master surgeons were manual workers rather than bookmen, but trained men were few and so the surgeons often encroached on the physicians' practice. The master surgeons of London were powerful enough to form a separate guild in 1368. Medieval knowledge of anatomy was dismal, because the Church had forbidden mutilation of corpses, and surgery of all kinds was very rough. Even so, surgeons trepanned skulls, operated on eye cataracts, hernias, and gallstones, using a scalpel with a grooved director to insure its steady path. Splints and plaster casts helped mend broken bones. Freedom from

A PHYSICIAN VISITS A NOBLE'S SICKROOM.

germs was a concern, despite the popular misconception that it was not. The surgeon washed his hands in boiled water and used sterile white of egg or strong wine on open wounds. The bleeding stumps of amputated limbs were cauterized with boiling oil or fire brands. For such painful processes there was an anesthetic made of henbane, hemlock, opium, meconium, mandragora, lettuce, and lard, mixed, boiled, and applied to the temples, palms, and soles of the patient. Doctors were not overly confident in their work, for they insisted on being paid before treatment, and heeded a distinguished colleague's advice not to "operate at all in any time when the operation is forbidden by the astronomers."

The domain of the master surgeons was invaded, in turn, by the low-class barber surgeons, who were cautioned not to take under their care "anyone under peril of death or maiming." Besides hair-cutting and hog-gelding, their specialties were blood-letting and cupping (cupping meant creating a vacuum over the afflicted area to make the blood rise to the surface). They performed the simplest type of surgery, like sewing up wounds, and sometimes they pitched in as dentists. Toothdrawer was the name of such a man, because the surest method of doing away with the worms that gnawed the roots of an aching molar was to extract the tooth. Those hurt in accidents did not generally have the best of care, for hospitals were dedicated to lepers, and the poor, old, and infirm. The usual way of dealing with an injured person was to take him to the nearest house, send for the priest, and hope for the best!

BARBER SURGEONS PERFORM AN AMPUTATION.

Home and Household

5

Just as there were rich people and poor people in Norcaster, there were rich houses and poor houses. The serfs who had newly bought their freedom and day laborers who had no land of their own rented rooms in tenements owned by the wealthy. Some were so poor they had no shelter but the open warehouses near the river. Others lived at the outskirts of town and outside the walls in narrow, two-room cottages not much different from a country peasant's. Two curved wooden uprights supported the roof beam and the walls, which were wattle and daub, or latticed with twigs woven around sticks and splattered with layers of mud and straw. The roofs were thatched and the floor was packed earth strewn with rushes that barely covered the rotting straw and refuse beneath. There was no chimney in any of these houses, and the fire in the middle of the room filled each of them with grimy soot, for little smoke escaped through the tiny shuttered windows or the chinks in the walls. Those who lived in these damp, dark, bare dwellings ate plain fare and slept on

118

straw. A dinner of bean soup, oatcake, eggs, salted herring, cheese, and ale was the most they could look forward to. A rabbit stealthily poached from the forest was a prize.

The shopkeepers and petty craftsmen combined their business and home life, usually in houses of two stories extending in solid rows down toward the marketplace. These dwellings consisted of a hall and bower, the hall divided by a low screen of wood, lath, and plaster from a rear passageway to a court. A chamber for sleeping and sitting was built at the other end, its long axis at right angles to the hall, so it presented its gables to the front. Most often the bower was raised above street level and had to be reached by a ladder or stair along the wall. The low room constructed beneath it served as a shop front, filled by day with noisy apprentices. At night the same space served as their bedchamber. In back, and separate, were the kitchen and storage buildings. There were other storerooms, of course, not only in the cellar, but also in the rooms above, where the householder kept provisions, utensils, and the materials of his trade. Sometimes he stretched sacks and bales across the rafters of the hall. The hoist that jutted out from most houses was used to haul up such heavy loads.

On the wider streets, at some distance from the

marketplace, stood the larger houses, belonging to those in the most lucrative trades—the victuallers, drapers, and mercers. These men provided the necessities of life to the town, and they took more than an honest profit from every townsman. The true merchant could afford to live in one place and transact his business in another, but he lived near the headquarters of his own guild, where his economic and political life centered.

The master draper's house was not the largest in town, but it was obviously the house of a well-to-do person. Large and sturdily built of lath, mortar, and stucco, it boasted the latest architectural ornaments, a gabled roof with a stag's-head finial, cross-timbered facade, and elaborate decorative carving on the doors and around the windows. The eaves and lintels were painted a bright tomato red.

The house stood within an enclosure guarded by a stone wall sixteen feet high. A heavy gate swung into the busy courtyard where chickens and children were always underfoot. By the gate, at the mayor's order, leaned a hooked pole, cords, and a hogshead of water. Fire was a constant threat in a town of open fires, thatched roofs, and party walls. The pole was to pull down the blazing thatch and the water to reinforce a cumbersome bucket brigade. The draper's family was fortunate not to have to depend

120

on the public conduits for their water supply, for there were few "standards" in the town, and it was a nuisance to send a servant to fetch water or pay for a carrier. The draw well in the center of the court and the cistern beneath the leaden roof gutter provided for their daily needs. By the larder house, which faced the court on the left, some newly pressed cheeses had been put out to dry. To the right was the garden, really an extension of the courtyard, a pretty place with fruit trees and tidy squares of flowers, vegetables, and herbs.

Across the courtyard, directly in line with the gate, was the entrance to the hall. A little roof

THE HALL DOOR

projected over the outer door, supported by fancy posts, with a balcony perched above. Security was a serious concern in those days of no banks, so it is not surprising that the oaken double doors were reinforced with iron and locked by a beam fitted across the inside into two metal slots. The inner door was fitted with a strong lock. During the day these doors and windows were closed fast against robbers.

Though it measured only 14 by 22 feet, the hall gave an impression of great space because of the high-pitched roof and scarcity of furniture. At one end was a passage to the parlor, and at the other an opening into a narrow corridor that led on the right to the buttery, left to the pantry, and ahead to the kitchen. The two rooms and garret above the pantry and buttery were used variously as workrooms, wardrobes, or sleeping chambers. Above the parlor was the solar or sun parlor—the master bedroom.

The draper's neighbor, the pelterer, had a smaller, more compact house. On the ground floor were a hall and a room with a chimney. Between the hall and the room was a larder, and over that a solar. A stable stood between the hall and the kitchen, with another solar above the stable and a garret above that. Like the majority of tradesmen, the pelterer used the narrow front of his establishment as a shop. Because his hall had no chimney, the fire was made on a flat hearth in the center of the room, and the smoke had to find its way out through a lantern in the tiled roof. At night the glowing ashes were swept into a *couvre-feu,* or curfew, a bell-shaped iron device cut out like a helmet. It kept the fire hot but safe until the morning.

The halls of both these houses were dark, even though the windows came right down to the ground. The panes were made of greenish glass, too coarse and thick to let much light through. In winter the heavy wooden shutters were closed against the cold, and the light had to come from the candlesticks and rushlights (tallow dips made from kitchen fat with rushes for wicks), which gave off smoke and an unpleasant smell with their flickering flame. In summer the shutters were lifted, the windows opened, and thrushes and magpies swung and chattered in front of the iron grating in their square wicker cages. Little pots of herbs were set out to bring a sweet smell into the hall. There was always need to sweeten the air, for the floor, though made of stone, was covered with rushes that were changed completely perhaps only twice a year. The new carpet strewn daily by the housewife and her maid only covered a mounting bed of refuse—food, bones, spit, vomit, and other waste from animals and their masters.

123

CUPBOARD

The furniture of the medieval hall was sparse. The draper owned two trestle tables, made of boards clamped together and placed on trestles. The tops could be lifted off and placed against the painted wall, as indeed they always were when not in use. Settles and benches with cushions, or bankers, were backed to one wall next to the carved oak cupboard, where the gold and silver plate was displayed during meals. On the floor next to it were the jugs, basins, and ewers that were used for washing hands. Several small stools with bankers were placed around the fireplace, the only comfortable-looking spot in the room. Perhaps the only beautiful thing was the oriel window with rich stained glass and tracery in the Decorated style. It was built out into a little bay with masonry seats, where people could sit face to face to chat and look into the courtyard.

In the vaulted cellar beneath the hall were casks and tuns full of wine and ale, apple cider, and perry, a cider made from pears. The buttery was a sort of wine cellar above ground where bottles were kept along with a few victuals. In larger households, the pantry was the domain of the dispenser. Here were stored the extra jugs and ewers, wooden earthenware and pewter platters, lanterns and candelabra, dishes and bowls with little silver feet, and shaggy linen towels and tablecloths. A typical burgher's house never contained an excess of furniture or even utensils. Forced moves were not uncommon in such uncertain times.

The larder was large because it had to hold a great deal. Some meat was eaten fresh, but the bulk was smoked, salted, or dried, and stored. There was no other way of preserving it. Such staples as grain, salted fish, lard, oatmeal, salt, and precious almonds were kept here too.

There were two fireplaces in the kitchen, one with a hood and chimney and another on an open

A BURGHER'S KITCHEN

hearth. The fire itself was all-important. There was a bellows to make it burn brighter and a damper to discourage it, but it was kept going all the time. The kitchen must have been a hot as well as a busy place. Caldrons sitting on iron tripods or hanging from an adjustable chain and hook bubbled over the flames while a full spit was hand turned over the coals. On the walls hung the frying pans and saucepans of brass and iron, trivet, tongs and griddle, sieve, strainer, and grater, and the fire-striking iron, in case the fire ever did go out. There were spoons for everything, for stirring and skimming and ladling, and a slice, or spatula, for turning the meat in the frying pan. Sausages ready for pot or pan hung limply from rods overhead.

The oval oven was built into the wall and it had a little arched roof overhead. It looked very much like a beehive. When the cook wanted to use it, he put a bundle of dry sticks inside, set fire to them, and closed the iron door. When the oven was properly heated, the door was opened, the ashes raked out, and the bread or pastries put in. When the oven was cold, the baking was done. Most of the household's bread was bought from the baker, but the housewife often had a little hand mill for grinding flour when she wanted to do some home baking.

On one side of the oven was a trestle table, with a

127

CORNER OF A BURGHER'S KITCHEN

dressing board and knife, and an ax. The butcher was usually responsible only for the killing of beasts. The carcass had to be hacked into chunks in the kitchen. The fowl had to be plucked and cleaned too. Sometimes a pig would be boiled whole, and there was a huge flesh hook for drawing such a large prize from the pot. Beside the meat board was a smaller one for chopping vegetables, also a mortar and pestle and a mier. The mier was used to crumble bread, and a larger mortar and pestle to mince and bray dozens of ingredients together to make the typical medieval dish. The idea was to mix a number of disparate elements into an unrecognizable whole. The greater the riddle the more successful the cook's art. Spices and herbs of every variety were kept in an open cabinet. Some, like rosemary, basil, sage, and thyme, came from the kitchen garden, and others were bought at great expense from the town spicer or at the yearly fair, but they served the same purpose—to make the stringy, salty, sometimes rotten meats palatable. The cook often flavored dishes with verjuice, the juice of crabapples or green grapes, and he kept a stone trough to crush the fruit. Water was stored in a large open vat in the corner of the kitchen.

Not far from the corner fireplace was the garde-robe pit, hollowed into a projection of the wall.

Kitchen waste, and perhaps other kinds, was thrown in here, later to be removed from the top by the kitchen boy. Outside the kitchen was a stone "house of ease-ment," or outdoor privy, which by town ordinance stood two and a half feet from the party wall.

The solar was not always an upper room, although its name derives from the Latin *solarium* or sun room. Sometimes the old bower or withdrawing room was called the solar too. Almost always, how-ever, it was used as the master bedchamber. The solar was bountifully furnished in comparison to the hall, because, if there was no parlor, the host often entertained his visitors there. The draper's solar was small, perhaps only 10 by 12 feet and was not even 8 feet in height. Despite its size it contained a bed, a cradle, a cupboard, benches, and a sizable chest at the foot of the bed. Like the furniture of the hall, that of the bedroom was handsome and sturdy, al-though hardly comfortable. The molded beams of the ceiling, the paneled walls, the woven hanging patterned with yellow fleurs-de-lis gave a certain warmth to the room, and certainly the bed behind the curtains looked luxurious enough for one of gentle blood. The rectangular frame was strung with rope from head to foot to hold a straw mattress, but over that was a soft feather bed and bolster covered with muslin sheets, a fur-lined coverlet, and a counterpane, its woven squares alternating yellow and blue. The bedstead itself was simple and could be made up into a couch by day. The ornate four-poster wasn't to make an appearance until the sixteenth century. The bedstead was placed under a canopy that extended half its length; the tester, or hanging in back of the bed, the canopy, and the curtains were hung from the ceiling. Bed curtains were very important to a medieval man. For one thing, they discouraged fleas, flies, spiders, and other pests. *The Goodman of Paris* lists dozens of methods of dealing with these sleep-stealers. It seems the fleas were the worst nuisance of all, but a scattering of alder leaves or a trap of bread smeared with bird lime was supposed to lure them to their doom. The curtains also kept the sleeper warm and closed him off from the "dangerous" night air. It was the custom to sleep naked, with nothing but a kerchief wrapped around the head.

For convenience there was a laver, or portable washstand that looked like a coat rack. One small bowl filled with soft, scented soap hung on the upper hook; the larger one below was for water. A linen towel was draped over the pole on the opposite side. There was a privy, too, with a chute to a pit in the cellar. On the open shelves of the cupboard, the draper kept some bronze ewers and pewter plates and two amber paternosters, beads for reciting the

131

WIFE AND DAUGHTER PREPARE A HOMEMADE
REMEDY FOR A BURGHER RESTING IN THE PARLOR.

Lord's Prayer. His furred clothes were kept safe in
the chest along with his other valuables, documents
and books, silver girdles, and jeweled rings and
brooches. It is hard to imagine that once an educated

132

man's library might consist of only five books, and that these had to be locked up; but before printing was introduced into Europe in the mid-fifteenth century, books were produced entirely by hand. Each one was hand lettered on sheets of parchment, sewn together and bound in wooden boards, then covered with leather and decorated. A book illustrated, or illumined, in tempera, silver, and gold could be a man's most precious possession. Daily apparel was hung on a perch, a wooden frame protruding from the wall. In a noble's household, another perch would be reserved for a peregrine falcon, and in some burghers' also, but the draper had no special taste for hunting and was not fond of falcons, though they were said to be "very tame, bold, and of good manners."

Another perch might have been used for hanging a lamp, which was nothing more than a linen or cotton wick floating in a bowl of oil. Lamp, candle, and flickering firelight added little light to the room, and candles were expensive to boot (tallow could cost four times the amount of lean meat). No wonder the burgher kept his hours by the sun. Probably as early as eight o'clock he snuffed out his candle, covered his fire, and "went to sleep with the hens."

At daybreak the watchmen on the towers blew the horn, and bells from churches in the four wards of

Norcaster rang out through the town. Once awake, the burgher washed his face, hands, and neck, and about once a month, or even more frequently, he took a bath. Doctors prescribed soaking in medicinal waters, but generally did not recommend opening the pores to the ravages of disease. Then, too, the typical medieval man was not known for fastidiousness. He may even have waited for a propitious conjunction of the planets to bathe himself all over, although it is certain that he bathed oftener than his eighteenth-century successors. It was the custom from the thirteenth century to enclose a wooden tub in a sort of tent made from linen drapes hung from a hoop fixed in the ceiling. Sometimes the bather sat in the tub, but another arrangement was to sit on the floor on a "greate sponge" surrounded by "litel sponges," dipping them in and out of a caldron of heated water. Privacy wasn't always the byword for bathing. The "stews" or public bathing houses in town were frequented by loose women; in fact, that probably was their main attraction.

The burgher dried with a shaggy linen towel and dressed before the fire on an herb-sprinkled sheet. First he put on a pair of loose drawers, then his long-sleeved linen shirt that fitted close over the arms and ended in cuffs over the hands. Over that went the paltock, or pourpoint or courtepy, as it was later called, a very short, tight-fitting tunic fastened down the front and buttoned from elbow to fingers and high about the neck. This was the newest version of the cotehardie, a longish tunic, which he could also choose to wear and belt low about the hips. The houppelande, often worn over the paltock, was a voluminous lined garment with flowing sleeves all dagged at the edges. It, too, was buttoned high at the neck.

Then, one by one, the burgher pulled on his chausses of two colors and tied them onto his paltock with white latchets. The chausses were breeches and hose combined, and at this period were parti-colored, made of motley, half red and half blue, or yellow and green—any combination was possible. The draper's girdle was silk and leather, studded with silver and buckled with gold. The girdle was a very fancy and expensive article. Its wearer had a choice of circling it about the waist or hips—the fashion changed every twenty years or so. Fastened to his girdle was the escarcelle or purse, quadrilateral in shape and usually of leather, tooled and ornamented. There were no pockets in those days, so everything a man wanted to carry with him had to be suspended from the girdle. A dagger or anelace jutted through one or both of the loops of the escarcelle. One sort of dagger was called a "misericorde" because it was used for the "stroke of mercy," a polite term for the death blow.

By this time the burgher's wife would have dressed her husband's hair (which was short and bobbed around the ears) with a bit of capon grease, shaped his forked beard with a comb of horn or ivory, and handed him his hat, shoes, and cloak. All kinds of headgear were worn at the end of the fourteenth century, from the merchant's Flemish beaver to the shaggy felt cap of the journeyman. The chaperon, or hood and cape combined, was a fashion so useful that it had been in vogue for centuries. In the 1300's, however, its peak had grown so long that it would have dragged in the street if it hadn't been tucked up under the girdle. The most popular hat among the well-to-do seems to have been the turban. This was really the old liripipe, or much-elongated chaperon, pulled up from where it dangled about the heels, and wound around a pad on the head, one end sticking out like a cockscomb. Another, and much simpler, hat was a pillbox with a rolled brim, rather high in the crown.

Extra length in clothes was fashionable then, as it often is in times of relative prosperity. The shoes were of soft leather with long and pointed toes. Called Cracowes, they were brought into fashion by the Polish courtiers of Anne of Bohemia, Richard II's first wife. An extravagant amount of material went into the houppelande, too. At the beginning of the fifteenth century the sleeves of the pourpoint bloomed into bagpipes, long at the elbow and tight at the wrists.

The streets were a menace underfoot and overhead, so the burgher wore wooden clogs with thick soles to raise him above street filth and an all-covering circular cloak for protection from refuse thrown out a window. Before he braved the streets, however, the burgher breakfasted lightly on bread, ale, and a bit of boiled beef. Then, if he were devout, he went to morning Mass and later to his place of business till the hour of dinner arrived.

While the master of the house was dressing, his wife made sure that he had clean linen and that his garments were warmed before the fire. Then she took up her polished metal mirror and attended to her own toilet. First she rubbed her teeth with green hazel or vinegar and a woolen cloth, and sweetened her breath with fennel. Then perhaps she put a bit of red color to her cheeks and lips, although such doings were severely reprimanded by the Church. She may even have dusted a bit of saffron in her hair (it seems blondes have always been envied) as she plaited it and wound it into tubes on either side of her head. Then she would tuck the plaits into a network of

MEN'S COSTUMES

MERCHANTS

WEALTHY
BURGHER

CITIZENS

BOWMAN OF THE
TOWN GUARD

golden wire, being careful that not a wisp showed. If her hair grew low on her forehead or neck she just plucked it out. Another style was to wind the plaits around the head, padding them with false hair if necessary before enclosing them in a stiff square caul of gold wire. At times the burgher's wife wore a wimple, a veil that fell down the back of her neck, or a gorget, a throat cloth that she attached to her hair with elaborate pins.

Her costume was simpler than her husband's, though its appearance changed a good deal oftener. One writer's complaint sounds all too familiar: "If a woman hears of a new fashion, she will never be at peace until she has the same." Often a wife's fashions aped her husband's. For instance, women quickly adapted the turban and houppelande to their own use. The usual garb consisted of a linen under-garment and a long tunic or cotehardie with sleeves buttoned tightly over the forearm and wrist. For warmth she might add a sleeveless woolen surcoat trimmed with fur. It was cut low to the thighs so that it showed her handsome girdle. An earlier style called for tippets, long narrow streamers of cloth that fastened like a cuff around the upper arm. Her skirts flowed full over her petticoat, though the bodice of the dress was fitted and rather high waisted. Her cloak, too, was of circular cut, but instead of always buttoning it over the right shoulder, as her husband did, she usually fastened it by a cord that passed through two loops in the backs of ornamental studs and then knotted at the waist.

A wife's day was as busy as her husband's. She may have joined him at Mass, worshiping in a separate pew, or attended a later service. In any event she spent more time in church than he did, if not always for pious reasons. It was no secret that she enjoyed the sermons of the traveling preachers. They were more like romances than sermons, filled with anecdotes of miracles that priests had culled from anthologies. Church-going then, as it is today, was

A BURGHER AT SUPPER

partly a social affair. By six in the morning the towns-woman was hard at the day's tasks, directing the maid to shake the featherbeds and bankers and change the baby's swaddling clothes. She herself put flowers in the hall and ordered the cook and scullion to prepare the dinner.

Dinner hour varied; sometimes it was at nine, sometimes at ten, or even as late as noon. Grace was said sometimes before the meal, and sometimes after, but the medieval Englishman was thankful at all times to tackle his bread, meat, and ale. His hands washed, the burgher sat at the table while the cloth was laid. Before him were his spoon in a case (he customarily used the knife he carried), an immense wooden goblet, a loaf of bread, and a trencher, a crustless slice of bread that was to be his plate. The trencher was made of bread four days old because it had to be hard enough to cut on. When the gravy seeped into it, the stale bread became quite palat-able, and if not eaten by the diner, was thrown to the dogs or given to the poor.

A medieval townsman's meals were hearty enough, but the variety never lived up to the promise of the cookbooks. An ordinary dinner consisted of a soup (131 different kinds are mentioned in one fifteenth-century cookbook); two or three plain dishes of meat, beef, mutton, and pork; a pastry, cheese, and fruit.

TABLEWARE

It was an age of stews and thick soups and strange flavors. Nuts and spices, sugar and salt, were mixed with meat, wine, and milk to make amazing pot-pourris. Blanc mange was a favorite dish, a concoction of meat or fish boiled with sweetened almond milk and served with sugar and salt. The recipes all call for sugar, but honey was the main sweetener. Sugar had to be imported and therefore was very expensive. Blandissory, first cousin to blanc mange, was a soup made with ground almonds and beef or fish broth mixed with pulped flesh and boiled in wine. The burgher was also fond of pasties, or meat pies. Something he called a "custard" was made like this: pieces of veal were boiled with a variety of herbs. Then into the pot went wine and a strange assortment of spices—cinnamon, cloves, mace, saffron. The meat was taken out and eggs beaten into the mixture, along with dates, ginger, and verjuice, and then it was all poured into the "coffyn" or pastry shell. The pastry was "endored" or glazed with saffron and egg yolks and baked. Another pasty filling would be pulped fresh pork mixed with eggs and strained. Pine nuts were added to this interesting combination and it was fried in lard, spiced with saffron, pepper, ginger, cinnamon, and salt, then poured into the coffyn with dates and raisins.

The recipe for mawmene ryalle called for a mixture of strong wine and powdered cinnamon, pine nuts, cloves, and almonds blanched and pounded. To this was added pulped brawn of capon, or failing that, hog's brawn (made with trimmings and boiled with herbs) mixed with ginger, salt, and more sweetened wine. All this was put in a pot to boil, and when ready to serve, the hodgepodge was colored with sandalwood, scattered with pomegranate seeds, pine nuts, and sugar, and served with a strong mustard sauce! Everything was washed down with a quantity of cider or ale.

Some attention was paid to table manners, though conduct approved in a medieval household would not pass muster with us. One writer admonished diners not to return morsels of food to the serving dish having had them in their mouths. The food was to be brought to the mouth with the fingers and never with the knife (forks had been invented but were not in common use until the seventeenth century), and no one should spit on the table. There were no restrictions about spitting on the floor. A fifteenth-century "Book of Nurture" counsels:

At the table behave thyself manerly,
not smacking thy lyppes as commonly do hogges
nor knawing the bones as it were dogges.

Pyke not thy teethe at the tabel syttynge
Nor use at thy meate over muche spytynge.

It was also good manners to wear a hat at the table, probably to keep stray hairs from falling into the dish.

Some took a nap after dinner, but a busy trader must have gone straightaway to his place of business, whether to the marketplace or Wool Hall or merely to the front of his shop. For the women who stayed at home there was spinning and stitching and mending, as well as tending the garden and minding husband, children, and household. The housewife knew how to stir up herb cordials and fruit syrups and make ink from gum, copperas, and gall. With soap made from potash, soda, and mutton fat, she did her washing in the river, beating it with a wooden paddle to make it clean. Stubborn stains were scrubbed in a solution of lye and fuller's earth or soaked in warm wine. To discourage moths she shook and sunned every garment and stored those not in use in a cedar chest full of bay leaves.

The medieval wife's main concerns were husband and children—in that order. The man was master of the house, and woman was subject to him in all things. When the Goodman of Paris advises his young wife to be modest and obedient, his tone is kindly, but we may be sure he would not hesitate to thrash her soundly if she didn't come up to snuff. The nurture of children must have been a precious duty to the medieval mother—she lost so many in childbirth and in early years.

Even though the goal for a boy was a good apprenticeship, his academic education was not neglected. Children of six or seven may have attended song school under Church jurisdiction, where they learned a few letters and words on sight. The song-school boy hung a hornbook from his belt, a sheet of parchment stretched over a wooden frame inscribed with an alphabet in the form of a cross and the paternoster. The sheet was covered with a thin sheet of horn. The youngster learned his Latin with the help of a psalter. The next step was grammar

BATHING A CHILD

school, where he learned to read, write, and do simple accounts, as well as to construe Latin into English. By the 1360's English replaced Norman French as the native tongue, and the children knew "no more French than their left heel." In Norcaster in 1387 the Corpus Christi Guild had established a free grammar school in the great Guildhall to help prepare youngsters for entrance into the universities. Up until this time education had been in the hands of the clergy. The school was still very small—only one master and twenty-five children. In grammar school the course was the *trivium* of grammar, rhetoric, and logic—

subjects to train the student to reason systematically and express himself clearly. The *quadrivium* of mathematics, music, geometry, and astronomy, along with the "natural sciences" of Aristotle were usually reserved for the university. Together the *trivium* and *quadrivium* made up the seven liberal arts. The medieval professor dictated from Latin texts, which the student learned by heart, graduating from Priscian's *Grammar* to Ovid, Horace, Cicero, and the Church fathers. A sign of proficient scholarship was to be able to debate in Latin and dispute a bold thesis against all comers. To win the degree of master in the university guild, the student, like any other ambitious craftsman, presented a "masterpiece"—a sample lecture. Six years was the normal course of study for master of arts, though several more were required for degrees in medicine, theology, and law.

If the housewife had any daughters, they helped in all the chores, at least until they were married. Although she had her daughters tutored at home, a mother's main duty was to look to their dowries and to marry them well and early. As a book of counsel advises her,

Busy thyself and gather fast for their marriage,
And give them to spousing as soon as they be
   of age.

Filial piety was considered the main virtue in those days, and severe discipline the best preparation for the difficulties of life. A recalcitrant child was beaten into submission by parents or schoolmaster:

> Take a small rod and beat them in a row,
> Till they cry mercy and their guilt well know.

Marriages were mostly matters of convenience for the parents, but for every two couples that did not exchange love-knots (as a sign of their devotion), there was probably one that did; and for every match of scold and tyrant, there were a goodly number of "married friends." Town girls were unlikely prospects for spinsterhood, but some nobles' daughters found a secure and often pleasant life in nunneries.

Not every wife was merely a housewife. The majority helped their husbands in the shop, and some even had businesses of their own, as their titles tell us—fishwife, alewife, brewster, bakester, spinster, and webster. Other responsibilities fell on a wife's shoulders during frequent absences of her husband on business, pilgrimages, or wars for his king, but she probably found the time to sit in the garden by the sundial and write him a letter or two.

The garden was the delight of any medieval household fortunate enough to have one. Nearly all the wealthy burghers had a town garden as well as land outside the walls that was tilled for their use. Even those less well-off could afford a few fruit trees in the backyard and a patch of cabbages, leeks, peas, as well as a variety of domestic garden herbs. Every household grew a few flowers, mostly violets, roses, lilies, honeysuckle, peonies, and daisies. The English are well known for their love of flowers. In medieval times they liked to wear garlands and chapelets or just wander among the blooms. The garden also grew all the vegetables the family used: peas, beans, cabbage, beets, turnips, lettuce, watercress, wild celery, fennel, borage, and garlic. The medieval housewife was expected to be a wise gardener—to know when to plant worts, as she called all vegetables, and how to prune and graft her fruit trees. We can imagine she did her best to keep the caterpillars from the cabbage patch by prayers and charms, without resorting to the sacrilege of breaking a consecrated Host over the leaves. Her fruit trees were apple, pear, warden, quince, and plum, and in some places in England walnuts, filberts, and chestnut trees were flourishing too. Her bushes bore strawberries and mulberries.

Herbs were grown not only to flavor food but also for their medicinal value. There was an herbalist in Norcaster, so the burgher's wife had no need for as complete a garden as her country counterpart's. But she may have looked to her cress to cure her husband's baldness or scurf, or smear wort to assuage his fevers. Asterion was supposed to cure falling sickness (epilepsy) but fervent prayers to St. Valentine were thought to be much more effective. Although to diagnose the imbalance of humors and to treat it was the doctor's business, both the apothecary and the housewife dabbled in practical and nonsensical preparations for the afflicted. Anyone who could read might find the semimagical recipe to ease difficult breathing: "Put the lung of a fox into sweetened wine and drink the mixture." Besides having recourse to St. Blaise, one might cure an inflamed throat by tying a magpie's beak around one's neck. There were also several ways to discover whether or not a patient would live. One of them was to "Give him lettuce and water, and if he spits it out, he shall not recover." Wifely concern, if it didn't save the patient, might at least avoid the doctor's bill, which was always astronomical.

An illustration of the early fifteenth century shows a man in a parlor stretched on a settle and warmly covered. His wife is reading from a book and stirring up a remedy for him. But this is rather a solemn scene for the parlor, which was, especially in the fifteenth century, to become a scene of warmth and gaiety. It was in this "little hall" that the master received important visitors, and here that the family often took its meals and played games after supper. The parlor was furnished more like the solar than the hall, except, of course, it had a settle rather than a bed; and in addition to the usual trestle tables and benches there was a chair. Tapestries hung on the walls that were not brightly painted with scenes from the Bible or a popular romance like "Alexander." The cupboard might hold the precious plate that the wealthy burghers were so fond of displaying. These vessels and ornaments of gold and silver were the medieval man's stocks and bonds, worth a great deal and easily convertible into ready cash. The parlor wall was the burgher's favorite place to hang his armor and lean his spear and shield.

Light came from the fireplace, candlesticks, and latoun chandelier (latoun was an alloy of brass much used in medieval times). Early ceiling lighting fixtures were candlebeams, or crossed beams of wood with a pricket on all four ends to hold tallow candles. The candlebeam could be lowered or raised by a hoist and pulley. The fireplace was smaller and cheerier than the one in the hall, and after supper the family would draw up benches or chests around it and tell stories. They also loved to dance and play games. In one special form of dance called the carol, the carolers held each other's hands and sang and danced in a circle, one giving time and tune to the rest. Everyone enjoyed music and there were few homes without a pipe and tabor, both popular and easy instruments to play.

The candlebeam could be let down to illumine quieter games like draughts, or checkers, tables, and chess. The tables looked like our backgammon board, and not surprisingly, one of the six or seven games played on the tables was "bagamon." The players threw the dice and moved counters along the points according to the count. Chess was the chess we play now, although the board was large and the pieces heavy. The winner had to beware a sore loser, because any one of the men thrown true could do considerable injury. Cards came into popularity in the fifteenth century, particularly when block printing was common. Forfeits and riddles could be a source of raucous amusement, and the coarser the joke the better it was received. In ragman's roll, each contestant drew a description of a "character" from a roll with a string, and then he had to behave as the roll commanded. Needless to say, the "character" was written in rude language. That was part of the fun.

A good many of the indoor games were of the rough-and-tumble variety. In blindman's buff, or hoodman blind, as the English called it, and in hot cockles, the blindfolded player was struck very hard and had to guess who his assailant was. In hot cockles the hand was placed behind the back to take the blow, but the "hoodman" had no idea where the blow was coming from. An illustration shows one poor fellow on the receiving end of a hefty swing with a heavy sack. These seem like childish games, but they were adult fare. Youngsters amused themselves with dolls, hobby horses, and whip tops.

At night the bells of Norcaster rang out again to sound the curfew. After that the taverners closed up shop and no person was allowed to walk about without a light. If they stayed up as late as ten, the burgher and his family wearily mounted the narrow stairs to the solar, a pet dog clambering after them, for a little sleep before another long day.

Feasts and Fairs

6

The townsman labored long, nine hours in winter, twelve hours in summer, but he counted the year's seventy-odd Sundays and holydays as times of revel, and lost no other opportunity to drink and carouse. The great landmarks of a man's life—birth, marriage, and death—were always occasions for ale-drinking, and even a solemn home vigil by a corpse's side might turn into a wild wake.

The merriest season was Christmastide, a festival that could last as long as a fortnight. Several saint's days were celebrated the week before Christmas; the Feast of the Holy Innocents fell on December 28; and Christ's baptism and the visit of the Magi were honored on Epiphany, January 6, the famous Twelfth Night of Christmas. It was a time of swiftly changing moods, of touching sentiment and wild license. Against a background of tender lullabies to the Infant Jesus erupted the Feast of Fools, when, under the scepter of the Lord of Misrule, the most dignified Church rituals were turned topsy-turvy. Yule logs burned in houses decked with holly and ivy, while mummers played and pranced in animal disguises. Townsmen exchanged gifts at the New Year, and on Twelfth Night they feasted on cakes and ale, drinking wassail with their neighbor at the table. Then as now special dishes were connected with certain times of the year. At Christmastide the wassail bowl was filled brimful with a concoction of ale, roasted apples, spiced cloves, ginger, nutmeg, and cinnamon, and the cakes, too, were full of spice. To drink wassail was a way of toasting a friend, calling for a formal exchange of bowls and a kiss. A succulent roast goose was a tradition at Michaelmas, just as we have turkey at Thanksgiving.

In ancient Britain many heathen ceremonials were closely allied with the agricultural turning points of the year. When Christ triumphed in the land, the Church, wherever she could, adapted pagan rites to her own use, and rechristened woodland gods as forces of evil—ogres, trolls, and goblins. The Feast of Christ's nativity conveniently coincided with immemorial celebrations of the winter solstice, honoring the sun's victory over darkness. Easter recalled ancient fertility rites signaling rebirth and resurrection. The pragmatic Church also turned festivals to her own profit, as at Hocktide, observed with the blessing of the first harvest of the winter fields. On

THE COOKS PREPARE COCKYNTRICE AND STUFFED
PEACOCK FOR A FEAST.

Hock Monday the women bound the men and demanded a money forfeit; on Hock Tuesday the men played turnabout, and the proceeds filled the coffers of the parish church. At Whitsuntide, or Pentecost, which went hand in hand with the Corpus Christi festival and fair, priests conducted Church ales, sisters to the town's scot ales.

Easter, following days of fast and penance, burst open the liturgical year with glory. Whitsuntide nearly always fell in May, and its religious ceremonies spurred a native joy at the coming of spring. May days meant an end to shivering dawns and long and dreary nights, the beginnings of walks in the woods and meadows to gather apple blossoms and whitethorn. At Whitsuntide Morris dancers traveled from hamlet to town, dressed in green and yellow motley, or disguised as trees. In each community they visited, they joined the townspeople in circling a beribboned maypole to such popular rounds as "Sumer is icumen in."

The bonfires and lanterns of St. John's Eve at the end of June echoed old customs of summer solstice. Of course everyone counted the days till Lammastide. If the summer harvest had been bountiful, not even the approach of winter could dim their spirits, and they saluted Martinmas with a jolly song.

It is the day of Martilmas
Cuppes of ale should freely passe,
What though winter has begun
To push down the shining sun.
                                    —*Anonymous*

By Corpus Christi, the Thursday after Trinity
Sunday, the great guild feast day of Norcaster, the
town had stepped into summer and all its delights.
Every holiday, and Corpus Christi was no exception,
was the occasion for dances, sports, and games of
every kind. Our medieval ancestors played most of
the games that are popular today, or at least some
form of them—quoits, kayles (nine pins), skittles,
bowling on the green, tennis, ice skating, soccer,
handball, and their favorite, archery. Sometimes
games were merely trials of strength, like wrestling,
weight lifting, throwing the hammer, or casting the
stone. The absence of written rules and umpires
guaranteed rough competitive sports. In fact, we
have learned much about them from coroners' rolls
(the borough court had to report violent deaths to
the crown). In one contest, usually confined to the
fairground, two blindfolded men were fastened by
ropes to a stake set in the ground, and armed with
clubs. Each man was free to circle the stake as far as

his rope would allow. A fat goose or pig was tethered to the same stake, and the object was to kill the squawking animal. Often enough, to the delight of spectators, the human participants knocked each other senseless.

Several sports required great skill as well as strength. Jousting was one of these, and even though tournaments were the domain of the nobles, young men of every station practiced feats of war. The countryfolk mounted on donkeys and tilted at cooking pots with broom lances. The town boys tested their skill at the quintain or in river battles. For quintains, a stout post was thrust into the ground and a short beam set on its top—like a capital T. The beam, which could pivot, was flattened and pierced through on one end. From the other, pointed, end hung a bag of sand. One would-be warrior tilted at the beam with a wooden spear, and if he hit the flattened end, the sandbag would swing around and hit his opponent. Fighting "battles" on the river Bure must have been exciting, if not dangerous. While a shield swung from a pole in midstream, an oarless boat fast approached, carried by the current. A young boy stood in the prow, ready to charge with his wooden lance. If he broke his lance, and didn't fall in, the youngster was "thought to have performed a worthy deede." More often he was

UG-OF-WAR   ANIMAL TRICKS   DANCING   STILT WALKING

ENTERTAINMENTS AT THE FAIR

dragged up the muddy bank to the tune of jeers.

Sport and games were put aside for the main events of the festival days, when the populace thronged the streets to witness processions, pageants, and miracle plays. In Norcaster there were two processions at Corpus Christi. One, secular in nature, took place on the eve of the feast, the other at nine the next day. Preparations became feverish as the day approached. Once-foul streets were cleaned by the rakers and made fragrant with rushes. The houses of the guild members were hung with purple, and doors opening onto the procession way were festooned with garlands of lilies, St. John's wort and orpin, feathery long fennel and green birch. Oil lamps swung in front of gates and torches seemed to blossom from the walls. The bonfires in the streets blazed as bright as on St. John's Eve.

The guildsmen marched two by two, bearing the arms of their crafts, the least important guilds leading the way. Behind them the town guard pranced on dapple-gray and bay mounts, their plate armor shining in the light of torches borne by the minstrels who flanked them. In the morning the crafts marched again with all solemnity, led by the mayor holding aloft the keys of the city. Other city elders in their official livery of red and white followed in pairs on richly caparisoned horses. Behind them came the craft guilds, this time in order of importance, preceded by wardens bearing white wands powdered with stars. It was easy to distinguish between the crafts, for each man had the emblem of his mystery embroidered on his sleeve, and the guild spearmen trailed belled pennants sewn with the craft insignia. A canopy shielded the two chief priests of the Corpus Christi Guild, who bore the precious Eucharist in a tabernacle of silver gilt, escorted by two choirboys with lighted guild candles. Behind these paraded other members of the council, bearing symbols of the Passion. Last of all came the pageants on carts tugged along by journeymen. The brightly costumed actors standing in dumb show promised days of entertainment to come. The procession made its way along a traditional path, from the marketplace, up High Street to Broadgate, then across to Aldgate, and back on Smithford Street to the Church of St. George, where the guildsmen offered candles and attended Mass. In the meantime the pageants pulled into place at their stations throughout the town, while half the populace pressed in for a closer look.

From nine to noon is a long time when one is used to eating at ten. The men returned to the guildhall with a good appetite for the feast. By custom, each guild held a banquet on its particular saint's day, and on other occasions as well, but sometimes the "feast" was nothing but bread and ale! In Norcaster, as we might have expected, no feast equaled the extravagance of the Corpus Christi Guild's on Corpus Christi Day. The leaders of the town welcomed the chance to show the wealth of Norcaster by feast as well as by procession and pageant. Whole oxen were brought in by the droves, and wine by the hundreds of barrels. The candles for the guildhall alone cost half as much as the provisions. It was an occasion grand enough for a king, and indeed Henry IV in the twelfth year of his reign had attended the festival. To avoid the unwholesome, bustling inn, he had stayed with a herbegeour, or official host, and the mayor had sent generous gifts of capon, pike, and ginger cakes, to show his gratitude for royal favor.

The day of the feast the guildhall was transformed. Gold banners floated from the hammerbeams, and the rushes had been swept from the floor to show the Malvern tile, glazed in green and yellow and decorated with white pipe clay in a bold geometric design. On the diapered wall, the heads of giant-antlered deer and wild boar alternated with rich hangings and wall torches. At the end of the hall was the dais or raised platform on which was placed a high-backed settle and the table dormant. This permanent table stood horizontally across the hall, while the other tables were stationed on trestles down the

164

hall's length. At the other end, above the screen that divided the hall from the kitchen area, was a balustrade called the minstrel's gallery.

The finest tapestry in the town belonged to the Corpus Christi Guild. It was Cloth of Arras, and the beauty of its representation of the Last Supper seemed to warm the cold and drafty hall. One huge fireplace was never enough to heat stone walls and tile floors, so the guests usually wore warm clothes. The array of this gathering dazzled the eye. There were silks and taffetas of every hue, dark velvets and lustrous brocades, trimmed with vair and ermine and embroidered with fine stitches. Jewels studded every girdle and turban, bells dangled from baldric and belt, and hands were heavy with rings. Some merchants were dressed in paltocks so quilted and puffed out they looked like pouter pigeons, others in houppelandes that trailed on the floor, and in crackowes so eccentric that the long toes had to be hooked by a golden chain to a garter below the knee! The retainers of the nobles were proudly decked in the livery of their lords, each in a distinctive color and heraldic emblems. One noble wife was dressed like a duchess

Preciously dight in diapered garments
In a surcoat of silk most rarely hued.
Wholly with ermine overlaid low to the hem

165

And with ladylike lappets the length of a yard
And all readily reversed with ribbons of gold
With brooches and bezants and other bright stones.
—*Alliterative Morte d'Arthur*

Some husbands and wives wore chapelets of flowers or coronals of golden wire, and on the wrist a favorite hunting bird, hooded and held by a leather strap called a jesse.

The guests were led to their places, served with water to wash from a bronze ewer, then seated each according to rank below or above the silver salt-cellar that stood at the center of the table to the right of the host. Also on the table was the nef, a silver vessel like a ship with a high prow and stern. The nef was usually filled with spices, although it is staggering to imagine anyone wanting to add a new flavor to the food.

When the food was about to be served, the minstrels struck up a tune. The services of these musicians were in constant demand during festival days. They played during procession, feast, pageant, and plays. Some towns, like Beverley, had their own minstrel guild, but Norcaster hired a wandering troupe. It was not until the mid-fifteenth century that the town acquired its own. The statuary group at Beverley

Minster shows only five musicians with vielle, fiddle, tabor, and several kinds of pipes. Undoubtedly the sculptor was limited by convention or lack of talent, for there were a number of instruments besides these, though not all were played in concert. A later medieval poem (*The Squire of Low Degree*) mentions most of them in a typical medieval catalogue.

> There was myrth and melody
> With harpe, getron, and sawtry,
> With rote, ribible and clockarde,
> With pypes, organs and bumbardes,
> With other mynstrelles them among,
> With sytolph and with sawtry song,
> With fydle, recorde and dowcemere,
> With trumpet and with claryon clere,
> With dulcet pipes of many cords.

That would have been quite an orchestra, if it ever existed. The poets of the Middle Ages were fond of indulging in long lists of things, just to show off their learning. An ensemble of thirty-six instruments mentioned in the fourteenth century is highly suspect. This poet has listed several string instruments: the guitar-like gittern (getron) and citole (sytolph), as well as the fiddle, psaltery (sawtry), rote, and ribible. The psaltery and dulcimer (dowcemere) were kinds of zithers like the mandore and

167

lute, the rote, a small, five-stringed harp, and the ribible, a harp-lyre. For some reason the portable organ was also called a dulcimer. The wind family was made up of pipe, recorder, shawm (oboe), and all the trumpets, clarion, bumbarde, horn, bugle, and buzine, as well as the rustic bagpipe. Percussives included the ever-present tabor or drum, tambourine, triangle, cymbals, bells, and clappers, although the poet mentions only the clockarde or chime bells.

Hired minstrels probably numbering ten at the most trooped down from the gallery to escort the servants who brought in the covered dishes of steaming pottage and juicy roasts on spits. The steward or dispenser bearing his rod of office led the way. At a grand feast like this, each person was served at his place, sharing his dish with a dinner partner. A carver carved before him, carefully holding the meat according to etiquette, with two fingers and a thumb.

Medieval feasts were usually served in three courses, and what courses they were! Each one consisted of ten or eleven dishes. We have a record of a banquet that could have been served in Norcaster to honor a royal visit. There may have been several more like it before festival days were over.

FIRST COURSE

Browet farsed, and charlet, for pottage.

MUSICAL INSTRUMENTS

Baked mallard. Teals, Small birds. Almond milk
served with them.
Capon roasted with the syrup.
Roasted veal. Pig roasted "endored, and
served with the yoke on his neck over
gilt." Herons.
A leche. A tarte of flesh.

SECOND COURSE

Browet of Almayne and viaunde rial, for pottage.
Millard. Roasted rabbits. Pheasant. Venison.
Jelly. A leche. Urchynnes (hedgehogs).
Pome de orynge.

THIRD COURSE

Boar in egourdouce, and mawmene, for pottage.
Cranes. Kid. Curlew. Partridge (all roasted).
A leche. A custarde.
A peacock endored and roasted and
served with the skin.
Cockagris (cockyntryce). Flampoyntes. Danyoles.
Pears in syrup.

Browet or brewet was a popular soup, and leche,
pulped pork cooked in a bladder, cut in the shape of
peapods, mixed with the "usual" spices and wine,

and boiled. Boar in egourdouce was the medieval version of sweet-and-sour pork. Flampoyntes were pork pies with points of crust sticking out. They made a conservative appearance in comparison to other coffyns complete with "wild werks," or fanciful pastry gargoyles. Serving a peacock in full plumage was an artistic feat. First the peacock was carefully skinned, head and tail left intact, and the carcass spread on a table and sprinkled with ground cumin. Peafowl could be stuffed in the normal manner, but one ambitious chef lined the peacock's body with a boned goose, and inside that poked a fat capon. A partridge followed the capon, and a quail the partridge. Finally a tiny lark was tucked into the quail, and the whole was roasted on a spit. When the fabulous bird was done, the brilliant feather skin was fitted over it, the tail displayed and a feather set blazing into the bird's gilded beak. That was a masterpiece to be carried triumphantly to the table.

Another fanciful dish may have eclipsed the glory of the peacock. The cockyntryce was created by interchanging parts of a capon and small pig. Scalded, skinned, and cleaned, each animal was cut in two across the middle and stuffed with pome de orynge (balls of pork liver mixed with spices) and then sewn to a new partner. The bird-animals were boiled, roasted on a spit, and before being served, glazed with egg yolks and powdered ginger. The dish acquired a garish look through marbling. The medieval passion for color invaded the kitchen too. Cooks used saffron for yellow, parsley or mint for green, and sandalwood or blood for red. Is it any wonder fresh tablecloths were *de rigeur* after each course? The soltete, or subtlety, a confection of sugar, jelly, and pastry which ended a course, gave the chef another chance to show his artistry. Some of these confections were unbelievably ambitious— St. George Slaying the Dragon, or The Trinity Watching Over the Virgin and Her Babe. They remind us of our modern ice sculptures, just as ornate and just as ephemeral.

It took several hours to eat one's way through all of this, and besides, during the long pause between courses, multi-talented minstrels played songs and recited romances and Breton lays, told vulgar anecdotes, juggled, conjured, and danced on their hands. The company stayed long at table after dinner, drinking piments (wine with honey and spices) or megethlin, sweetened mead. Hippocras, wine strained and spiced, was served with dessert and wafers, sugar plums, marzipan, and ginger cakes. As one medieval alliterative poet tells us:

There were claret and Crete wine in clear silver fountains

Wine of Alsace and Antioch and Hippocras
  enough,
Vernaccia from Venice, wine of great virtue,
Rhenish wine and Rochelle, and wine from Mount
  Rose

Spices (desserts) were dispensed with unsparing
  hand,
And Malmsey and Muscatel, those marvelous
  drinks,
Went readily round in fair russet cups.

Hippocras was the drink usually reserved for the
mazer, a bowl of bird's eye or spotted maple,
rimmed, ornamented, and footed in silver, and passed
around like a loving cup.

In the afternoon all eyes were on the pageants
and miracle plays, those dramatic scenes from the
Bible so fervently presented by the guildsmen of
Norcaster. For most medieval people, information
came through sight and sound, through a story
told by the fire, or a rousing sermon acted out by
the parish priest, from a fresco or stained-glass window in a church, or even a shop sign. The drama,
which combined imagery, words, music, and action,
could teach and delight at the same time, and so
it did from its earliest beginnings in the Church
ritual. The Church had always wooed her people

this way, and she offered the budding drama some equally important props—an altar as a stage, vestments for costumes, and a choir for music. Her congregation was a captive audience. From the tenth century onward, particular incidents in the Old and New Testaments were singled out for performance at special feasts. On the Feast of the Holy Innocents, choir boys fell down in a heap at the foot of the altar, as if slaughtered by Herod's soldiers, then rose and mounted into the Sanctuary, which represented heaven. At Easter especially, tropes or embellishing texts to accompany music were added to the traditional liturgy. Invented dialogues like the *Quem Quaeritus* between the Marys and the angels at Christ's empty tomb became our first recorded "plays."

Representation was always an explicit part of the drama, and increased splendor of dress and detail of speech and gesture quickened dramatic development. As performances became more and more elaborate—and irreverent—the drama moved out of the church into the churchyard, and from there into the marketplace and street. In Norcaster, as elsewhere, the miracle play, as it was now called in England, gradually passed from the hands of the clergy into the hands of the people. The cycles of plays grew long, beginning with the Creation and ending with the Last Judgment. Pageants could number as many as forty-two. Norcaster's twenty-four pageants were the responsibility of the craft guilds, some of which were rich enough to provide for an entire pageant, while lesser guilds banded together to produce theirs. If it could be managed, each guild was charged with a subject allied to its craft. To the bakers went the Last Supper, to the vintners, the Miracle at Cana; Noah and the Ark fell to the fishmongers or shipwrights, and the goldsmiths presented the Magi. The cooks were given the Harrowing of Hell, perhaps because the heat of their shops and wide-mouthed ovens suggested the infernal gate.

The town council watched the crafts closely so they would be sure to carry out their multitudinous duties, like gathering properties and costumes, revising plays and copying the script, as well as providing refreshments before and after the play and paying the minstrels, actors, and prompters. The pageant pence that paid for all of this was an obligation on all guildsmen. Unless there was a special pageant house, properties were kept from year to year in the guildhall, being added to or replaced just before the festival. Adam and Eve had a tree of knowledge, Judas his bag of gold, and God a papal tiara. The sound-effects department needed a barrel to make thunder and brass pots for a general clatter. Actors' fees were generous, and "God" received suitably more for his work than the "Worms of Conscience." Auditions for talent came next, and a committee decided who was to play God, and who the devil, both less demanding roles than that of wicked King Herod. When any bright clerk revised a play, he usually added something new, especially a comic scene, or character, like Noah's shrewish wife, though the inexperienced found it hard to find a meter appropriate to drama. Naturally, several rehearsals were needed to ready the play in time for the Corpus Christi procession.

The pageant wagons that followed last in the procession were really movable stages. There was no open space in the town large enough to accommodate all the spectators, so the plays were brought to them. Each open cart had two sections, upper and lower. For the most part, the action took place on the upper level, which could be seen from both sides. The lower, with curtains closed, was used as a dressing room. The actors could descend through a trapdoor unseen, change costumes and clamber up again to declaim in a new role. Sometimes the curtains opened to show a hell mouth below, heaven above. Sets were simple but tremendously effective, in a mode part naturalistic, part surrealistic. The hell mouth was a gape-jawed dragon's head. Jowls snapped and eyes rolled, while fire, smoke, and a jangle of pots and pans issued from within.

The plays began in the afternoon, the pageants creaking from station to station to repeat each performance, while minstrels played between scenes. The townsmen knew the stories by heart, so the interest lay in the presentation of the scene. Within the limits of story, stage, and literary convention, clever clerks found springboards to action. They created comic interludes with secondary characters, or even new ones, rooting their material in common life and appealing to a gamut of emotions—tender sentiment, awe, terror, and raucous humor. Mary Magdalene was a contemporary prostitute with rough talk and fancy clothes. Noah's wife was the easily recognizable shrew of the *fabliaux*, who, denied mastery of the house, lashed her husband with her tongue. The scene goes like this: when everyone is in the ark, Noah's wife is still fussing about the domestic arrangements. When the flood's really at hand, an exasperated Noah tells her she can do what she likes. Finally she goes in, but gets a cuff on her ear for the trouble she's caused, to the joy of the male members of the audience.

The audience's favorite villain was the arrogant Herod with painted face and turban, who swore by

177

Mohammed that he had come "alle yonge children to slay." It was a great role, calling for "raging," that is, brandishing of sword and stomping of feet and a bellowing voice that boomed out,

> I am the cause of this great light and thunder.
> [*A guildsman beats a barrel from below*]
> It is through my fire that they such noise do make,
> My fearful countenance the clouds do so encumber
> That often for fear therof the very earth does quake.
>
> —*The Play of Herod*

Hard on the heels of the plays followed the fair. On the brow of the hill a wooden town had sprung up, guarded by a timber palisade and locked gates against thieves and dishonest traders who might try to smuggle in their wares free of toll.

The semiannual fair of Norcaster was not a great fair like those on the Continent, nor could it even compare with Stourbridge Fair at Cambridge, or St. Giles at Winchester, both of which lasted three weeks. But the wealth and excitement it brought the town in six days did last—at least until the next fair.

The fair was a valuable source of revenue. Rents

and fees on every sale went into the town's treasure chest, and the council made sure that all shops were closed so trading was done at the fair. Of course the swell of population in residence brought a harvest of money to nearly everyone. Excitement mounted as caravans of carts and teams of sumpter beasts laden with panniers arrived exhausted at the fair. The way had been long and arduous. Some had not arrived at all, for the broad-bottomed boats of the merchant adventurers fell easy prey to pirates on the high seas. Once on the road, the merchants had to contend with town tolls and a jumble of local laws and currency, traveling in constant fear of robbers. They even had to carry food and fodder, for roadside inns were few and far between. An alestake was a welcome sign at a crossroads. Since Roman days roads had fallen into disrepair. Many of them were no more than grassy tracks full of ruts and dangerous pits. The square, flat-sided carts sat tall on two gigantic wheels to ride the deepest furrow and straddle the highest ridge.

When the last caravan unloaded at the fair site, beasts were tethered and fed, and merchants took stock of a familiar scene. The fair was laid out in streets like a town, but this was a canvas village, and shops were tents propped up over counters piled high with goods. Here were lengths of shimmering silks from Italy, rare spices from the East, wax and tapestries from the Netherlands and France, armor from London, dried fruits and nuts from Spain and Italy, furs from the Hanse towns, pitch and charcoal from the Baltic. Local goods were exchanged as well, for bailiffs came from far to sell surplus from manor farms and stock their larders for the year. Certain days were set aside for the sale of such English goods as hides and metalwork.

When pennons flew from every tent-top, a trumpet blast signaled the opening of the fair. The mayor of Norcaster proclaimed a welcome to all and counseled everyone to honor the peace, keep holy the Sabbath, and abide by the rules of the fair. He did well to warn the crowd, for the peace and rules of the fair were broken often enough. Some sharpster always drove too hard a bargain, or an innocent was robbed by a cutpurse. The special court that was set up to deal with the transactions and troubles arising from the fair was called piepowder, from the French *pied poudré*, a reference to the dusty feet of the merchants who trafficked there. Piepowder held authority only during fair days and provided a kind of instant justice in which the cause was presented, complaint heard, and judgment delivered and executed in the same day. The merchants carried a customary law with them from fair to fair, which came to be known as the Law Merchant. The difference in currencies was always a headache. An enormous number of transactions were made on paper, and the piepowder court sometimes acted like a bank at fair's end, settling accounts between Italian and Lowlander, Spaniard and Englishman.

The crowd was just as intent on merrymaking as on trading. The ordinary townsman was a spectator along with the minstrels and tumblers, beggars and preaching friars. A throng of pleasure-seekers mingled with quacks and drug sellers, chapmen and pedlars, and pardoners with false relics as they picked up a fast penny from bystanders at the amusements. As diversions to serious trading, bears performed to pipe and tabor—in answer to a firm tug on a chain—fierce dogs baited bulls in a ring, strongmen wrestled or chased a pig around a stake, while Punch cracked Judy again and again.

The laughter faded in the later fifteenth century, or at least changed its abode. By the 1500's the fair site was filled with permanent dwellings and the miracle plays had been pronounced too expensive to produce. In a hundred years Norcaster had changed in so many ways that it was no longer a "medieval" town.

Bibliography

Abram, A. *English Life and Manners in the Later Middle Ages.* New York, 1913.

Addy, Sidney Oldall. *The Evolution of the English House.* Social England Series, edited by K. D. Cotes. London and New York, 1898.

Anson, Peter F. *The Building of Churches.* New York, 1964.

Bagley, J. J. *Life in Medieval England.* London, 1960.

Bennett, H. S. *Life on the English Manor.* Cambridge, 1938.

Besant, Walter. *Medieval London,* Vols. I and II. London, 1906.

Calthrop, Dion Clayton. *English Costume.* London, 1926.

Cambridge Medieval History, Vols. I–VIII. New York, 1936.

Chambers, E. K. *The Medieval Stage,* Vol. II. Oxford, 1925.

Coulton, G. G. *Chaucer and His England.* Cambridge, 1935.

———. *Life in the Middle Ages.* Cambridge, 1932.

———. *The Medieval Village.* Cambridge, 1926.

———. *Medieval Panorama*. New York, 1938.

Crump, C. G., and Jacob, E. F. (eds.). *The Legacy of the Middle Ages*. Oxford, 1926.

Cutts, E. L. *Colchester*. Historic Towns Series, edited by E. A. Freeman and W. Hunt. London and New York, 1886.

———. *Scenes and Characters of the Middle Ages*. London, 1930.

Davis, William Stearns. *Life on a Medieval Barony*. New York, 1951.

Derry, T. K., and Blakeway, M. G. *The Making of Britain: Life and Work to the Close of the Middle Ages*. London, 1968.

Documents Illustrating the History of Civilization in Medieval England (1066–1500), translated and edited by R. Trevor Davies. New York, 1948.

Evans, J. *English Art, 1307–1461*. New York, 1949.

Flinn, M. W. *An Economic and Social History of Britain, 1066–1939*. New York, 1961.

Gies, Joseph and Frances. *Life in a Medieval City*. New York, 1969.

Green, Mrs. J. S. *Town Life in the Fifteenth Century*, Vols. I and II. New York, 1895.

Gross, Charles. *The Gild Merchant*, Vol. II. Oxford, 1964.

Hartman, Gertrude. *Medieval Days and Ways*. New York, 1968.

183

Hartley, Dorothy, and Elliot, Margaret M. *Life and Work of the People of England: A Pictorial Record from Contemporary Sources.* Vol. II, *The Fourteenth Century;* Vol. III, *The Fifteenth Century.* New York, 1929.

Hassall, W. O. (comp.). *How They Lived: An Anthology of Original Accounts Written Before 1485.* Oxford, 1962.

Hole, Christina. *English Home-Life 1500 to 1600.* London, 1947.

Holmes, Urban Tigner, Jr. *Daily Living in the Twelfth Century. Based on the Observations of Alexander of Neckam in London and Paris.* Madison, Wis., 1952.

The Horizon Book of Great Cathedrals. New York, 1969.

The Horizon Book of the Middle Ages. New York, 1969.

The Horizon Cookbook and Illustrated History of Eating and Drinking Through the Ages. New York, 1968.

Houston, Mary G. *Medieval Costume in England and France.* A Technical History of Costume Series, Vol. III. London, 1939.

Huizinga, J. *The Waning of the Middle Ages.* New York, 1938.

Jusserand, J. J. *English Wayfaring Life in the Middle Ages.* New York, 1950.

Lacroix, Paul. *Science and Literature in the Middle Ages—and the Renaissance.* New York, 1962.

———. *Military and Religious Life in the Middle Ages—and the Renaissance.* New York, 1962.

Lamont, A. *World of the Middle Ages.* New York, 1950.

Langland, W. *The Vision Concerning Piers the Plowman,* edited by W. W. Keats. Oxford, 1886.

Lincoln, E. F. *The Medieval Legacy.* New York, 1946.

Loomis, Roger Sherman, and Willard, Rudolph. *Medieval English Verse and Prose in Modernized Versions.* New York, 1948.

Low, Professor A. M. *England's Past Presented.* New York, 1953.

Lunt, W. E. *History of England.* New York, 1947.

McKisack, May. *The Fourteenth Century: 1307–1399,* in *The Oxford History of England,* edited by George Clark. Oxford, 1959.

Mead, William Edward. *The English Medieval Feast.* Boston, 1931.

National Geographic Society. *The Age of Chivalry.* Washington, 1969.

Norris, Herbert. *Costume and Fashion.* Vol. II, *Senlac to Bosworth, 1066–1485.* London, 1927.

Painter, Sidney. *Medieval Society.* Ithaca, N.Y., 1951.

Pirenne, Henri. *Economic and Social History of*

Medieval Europe, translated by Paul Kegan. London, 1936.

———. *Medieval Cities,* translated by Frank D. Halsey. Princeton, 1925.

Power, Eileen (trans. and ed.). *The Goodman of Paris.* London, 1928.

———. *The English Wool Trade in English Medieval History.* London, 1941.

———. *Medieval People.* New York, 1962.

———, and Postan, M. M. *English Trade in the Fifteenth Century.* London, 1938.

Prendell, Charles. *London Life in the Fourteenth Century.* London, 1925.

Quennell, Marjorie and C. H. B. *A History of Everyday Things in England.* Vol. I, *1066–1499.* London and New York, 1968.

Rickert, Edith (comp.); Olson, Clair C., and Crow, Martin M. (eds.). *Chaucer's World.* New York, 1942.

Rickert, N. *Painting in Britain: The Middle Ages.* Baltimore, 1954.

Rorig, Fritz. *The Medieval Town.* Berkeley, 1967.

Salzman, L. F. *English Industries of the Middle Ages.* Oxford, 1923.

Stephenson, Carl. *Borough and Town: A Study of Urban Origins in England.* Cambridge, Mass., 1933.

Stone, L. *Sculpture in Britain: The Middle Ages.* Baltimore, 1955.

Traill, R. *Social England.* London, 1938.

Trevelyan, G. M. *Illustrated English Social History.* Vols. I and II. New York, 1949.

Webb, G. *Architecture in Britain: The Middle Ages.* Baltimore, 1956.

Wright, Thomas. *Homes of Other Days.* London, n.d.

Index

accounting, 31-32
agriculture, 88
   three-field system of change
     to, 12
aldermen, function of, 56-57
ale, 93
   control of price of, 59, 93
Alexander of Neckham, 6
anatomy, ignorance of, 114
animal tricks, 161
apprenticeship, 51-53
archaeology, 6
architecture:
   church, 26-28
   of draper's house, 120
   masons and, 62
armor, 24, 70-72
"assent and consent," 55
Assize, Great, 109
assizes:
   Clarendon, 109
   control of price and quality
     by, 58-60, 92-93
   definition of, 110
Assize of Arms, 24
astrology, 112
attack, methods of, 22
aulnager, function of, 87
Austin Canons, 16, 26

bailiffs, function of, 56-57,
   108

bakers, 58-59, 60, 91-92, 95
barber surgeons, 114, 116,
   117
barbicans, defensive function
   of, 22
basketweaver, 53
bathing, 134, 147
bedroom, burgher's, 130-133
Beverley Minster, 166-167
Black Death, 8
blacksmiths, 70-73, 96
boatmaker, 35
books as prized possessions,
   132-133
"Books of Nurture," 3, 145
boroughs, royal, 40
Bracton, Henry de, 110-111
brass, workers in, 73-74
bread:
   regulations regarding, 58-
     60, 92
   types of, 91-92
brewing, 93
Brut (Layamon), 4
burgesses, 41, 54
butchers, 88, 89-90
buttery of burgher's house,
   125

Cambridge, 178
Canterbury Tales, The
   (Chaucer), 1-2

188

dancing, 152-153, 158, 161
Danelaw, 20, 103, 109
day laborers, living conditions of, 118-119
defense, town, 19, 21-26
dentistry, 116
disciplining of children, 149
diseases, prevalent, 113
Domesday Book, 40-41, 54
drama, evolution of, 173-178
drapers (*see also* waster draper), 87, 88, 95, 120-122
dress:
    burgher's, 135-137
    burgher's wife's, 137-141
    for Corpus Christi feast, 165-166
    men's, 138-139
dyeing, 85-86

Easter, 158, 174
education, academic, 146-148
Edward I, King, 106
Edward II, King, and cloth industry, 79-80
Edward III, King, 4, 20, 24
    cloth industry and, 78-80
    Parliament and, 107
ember days, 90
equity, 105
Exchequer, Royal, 31, 105

fabliaux, 2-3, 177
fair, Norcaster's:
    description of, 178-181
    right to hold, 44
    as source of revenue, 179

farm of the borough, 57
    meaning of, 41-42
Feast of Fools, 155
fire precautions, 120
fish, available types of, 90-91
fishing, freshwater, 14
fishmongers, 88-89, 90-91
fishvendors, 91
Fistula in Ano (John of Ardene), 3
Flanders and the cloth industry, 78-80
Flesh-Shambles, 89-90
flowers, garden, 121, 150
Franciscans, 16-17, 26
frankpledge, 103
free status, conditions of, 37
Froissart, Jean, 4
fruit, garden-grown, 150
fulling, 81, 84-85
furniture:
    bedroom, 130-133
    hall, 124-125
    parlor, 150-152

gambling, 94-95
games:
    indoor, 153-154
    outdoor, 159
garden, burgher's, 121, 149-151
gates, town, 20-22
gold beaters, 76
goldsmiths, 74-77
Goodman of Paris, 3, 131, 146
Gower, John, 2, 99
grammar school, 147-148
Grayfriars, 17

grocers, 47, 88, 95-96
guildhall, Norcaster's, 29, 61,
    66
  on Corpus Christi Day,
    164-166
guilds (*see also* Corpus
    Christi Guild):
  charitable, growing power
    of, 48
  craft, rise of, 46-47, 49-54,
    80
  decline of democracy in,
    53-54
  division of labor and, 50-
    51
  feasts of, 163-164
  masons', 62
  merchant, 43, 45-46, 49,
    80
  miracle plays and, 175
  Norcaster's, 48
  town council and, 48

hall of medieval house, 121,
    123-124
Hastings, 39
Henry I, King, 24
Henry II, King, 42
  common law and, 104,
    109
Henry IV, King, 107
Henry V, King, 107
herbs:
  garden, 121, 150-151
  medicinal use of, 150-151
Higden, Ranulf, 4
Hippocras, 173
Hocktide, 156-158
Holy Innocents, Feast of, 174
housewives, 137-141, 145-146

businesses of, 149
  remedies of, 132, 151
"hue and cry," 57, 98, 108
humors, bodily, 113-114
hundreds, 41, 109

illumination, 5, 133
inns, 17-18
  roadside, 79
Inns of Court, 111

Jews, eviction from England
  of, 32
John, King, 40
John of Ardene, 3
joiner, 71
journeymen, 51-53
  associations of, 54
jousting, 160
jury system, 108-110
justice, *see* courts; law
justices, king's special, 42,
  57, 108, 109

keep, Norcaster's, 26
King's Bench, Court of the,
  105
King's Council, *see* Curia
  Regis
kitchen, burgher's, 125-129
knifemaking, division of labor
  in, 70

Langland, Will, 2
larder of burgher's house,
  125
law (*see also* courts):
  canon, 100-102
  common, 3, 5, 104-111
  feudal, 102-104

191

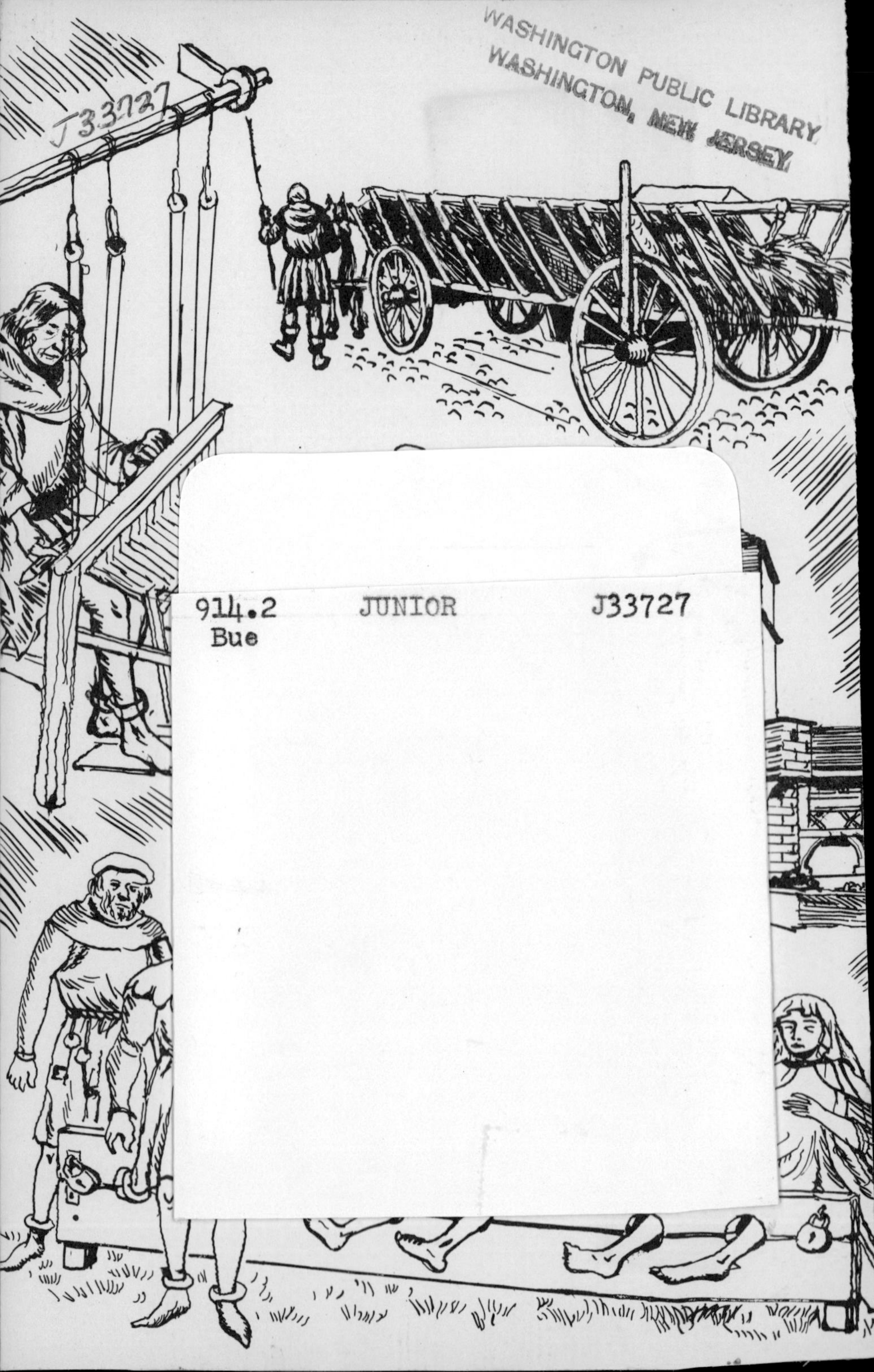